A FRESH LOOK AT CHESS

40 instructive games,
played and annotated by players like you

with comments by Grandmaster
LEV ALBURT

Also by Lev Alburt

Comprehensive Chess Course
(From Beginner to Master and Beyond)

1) *Learn Chess in 12 Lessons*
2) *From Beginner to Tournament Player*
3) *Chess Tactics for the Tournament Player*
4) *The King in Jeopardy* (The Best Techniques for Attack and Defense)
5) *Chess Strategy for the Tournament Player*
6) *Chess Training Pocketbook* (300 most important positions and ideas)
7) *Just the Facts!* (Winning Endgame Knowledge in One Volume)
   Chess Journalists of America 2001 Book Of the Year!

Companion Volumes

8) *Chess Training Pocket Book II* (320 key position for players of all levels. How to spot tactics and how far ahead to calculate) A sequel to Volume 6.
9) *Building Up Your Chess* (The Art of Accurate Evaluation and Other Winning Techniques)
10) *Chess Rules of Thumb*
11) *Three Days with Bobby Fischer and other chess essays* (the living history of chess, told by one of its makers)

Every chess player needs a set of openings he can trust!

12) *Pirc Alert!* (A complete defense against 1. e4)
13) *Chess Openings for White, Explained* (winning with 1. e4); a.k.a. *White Book*
14) *Chess Openings for Black, Explained* (the complete repertoire, based on the Hyper-Accelerated Dragon and Nimzo- Bogo complex); a.k.a. *Black Book*

Volumes 13 and 14, besides presenting a reader with a complete, interconnected repertoire, also provide a very practical overview of all openings, from the White and Black point of view respectively.

15) *Chess for the Gifted and Busy* (a short but comprehensive course from beginner to expert)

Since the first two volumes appeared in 1986, Lev's books have been constantly revised and updated. E.g., Volume One is currently in its Fifth, Enlarged edition.

Lev's Co-authors:
FM and FIDE Senior Trainer Roman Pelts (1,2); GM Sam Palatnik (3-5); GM Nicolay Krogius (7); Expert and CJA 2001 Journalist of the Year Al Lawrence (8, 10, 11, 15); GM Alex Chernin (12); GMs Roman Dzindzichashvili and Eugene Perelshteyn (13-14).

In the text of this book all references to these titles are in **bold**. For more information and how to order, see pages 222-224.

Chess Information and Research Center
P.O. Box 534, Gracie Station, New York, NY 10028
212-794-8706
For ordering information, see last page.

Library of Congress Control Number: 2011940902
ISBN 978-1-889323-25-1
Distribution to book trade:
W.W. Norton, 500 Fifth Avenue, New York City.

Printed in the United States of America
10 9 8 7 6 5 4 3 2 1

To my parents

TABLE OF CONTENTS

*For ratings (shown here in brackets) see page 9.

Introduction

Some chess books are written by Grandmasters to serve (or to impress) their peers. Many more have been written by Grandmasters (and occasionally Masters) to help untitled players (aka Amateurs, encompassing both beginners and experienced club players alike) to understand and to play chess better, using positions and games taken from other Grandmasters' (often World Champions) practice.

What can an average Joe learn from games played by Jose (Capablanca) or Garry (Kasparov)? After all, he doesn't have Capa's intuitive feeling where to place his pieces; neither can he calculate flawlessly many moves ahead as Kasparov routinely did. The answer is: "A lot" — as long as the positions and games have been well selected and well explained. Still another — not exclusive, but complementary — approach to chess studies, namely learning from errors and successes, problems and thoughts of players like yourself, is worthwhile, too.

Some coaches-turned-writers, like myself, used this approach, and their students' practice, in their books— usually as an extra, as icing on the cake.

However, for the last ten years, I have been in a unique position, writing a very special column for *Chess Life*, the official publication of the U.S. Chess Federation and the most widely circulated (70,000) chess magazine in the world. Untitled readers are invited to send me their most instructive and well-annotated games. Every month I choose, from a dozen or more entries, the one I deem most instructive for the majority of readers and publish it, with comments and advice, in that column.

For this book, I selected 40 most instructive columns, arranged them by theme, cut some material — and added much more, all to make it both instructive and fun to read and learn from. Of course, the thematic division may go only so far. For instance, games of child prodigies are likely to include elements like tactics, traps, attacks, endgames . . . And while I corrected misspellings and other obvious errors, I did not edit (except for cuts) contributors' texts: I want them to speak to you in their own voices, and not in mine!

I'm very grateful to my Chess Life *editors: Dan Lucas,*
Jo Anne Fatherly, Alan Kantor, and Ron Burnett,
and to former editors,
Peter Kurzdorfer, Glenn Petersen, and Kalev Pehme,
for their help and guidance

Some Explanations

Ratings

Four-digit numbers next to players' names are U.S. Chess Federation (USCF) ratings, which reflect each players' recent performances. A relative beginner is usually rated somewhat below 1000. *Class E:* 1000-1200; *Class D:* 1200-1400; *Class C:* 1400-1600 (the median rating of USCF members is around 1600); *Class B:* 1600-1800 (my contributor's rating, at the time he played the submitted game, should be under 1800); *Class A:* 1800-2000. Now, titles: *Expert:* 2000-2200; *Master* or National Master (NM): 2200-2400; *Senior Master*: over 2400.

The International Chess Federation (FIDE) has it's own rating system; usually, USCF's ratings are slightly higher (for instance, 2500 FIDE is probably 2560 USCF). FIDE's titles are based on certain tournament results, not directly on ratings. Still, we can say that an *International Master* (IM) is rated 2400-2550, and an *International Grandmaster*, or simply Grandmaster (IGM or GM) is rated 2500 and up, with one or two reaching, at times, somewhat above 2800 (There is some inflation of ratings; in the early 1980s, then-World Champion Anatoly Karpov, and only he, was rated above 2700).

The difference in ratings indicates *predicted results*. For instance, in case of 100 points difference, a six-game match should end 4-2 in favor, of course, of the stronger (higher rated). In this case, they both keep their ratings unchanged.

***ECO* Codes**

A letter and a two-digit number in brackets following the name of an opening is a code for a certain variation (line) of a chess opening, as used by the *Encyclopedia of Chess Openings (ECO)*.

Time Controls

In a serious tournament, each player is given two hours to make his first 40 moves (or 90 minutes for the first 30 moves), then — one hour — for the rest of the game. Game/one means each has only one hour for the entire game; Game/30 — 30 minutes. (These contests, and those below, are also called *Sudden Death*). Controls like 30 or 20 minutes per game are called *Rapids*; less than seven minutes per game — *Blitz*.

Sometimes, *increments* of 2-30 seconds are added after each move, to alleviate time scrambles.

The Symbols

+/=, +/-, and +- mean small, large, and decisive advantage for White; -/=, -/+, and -+ mean the same for Black. (!?) means "interesting move"; (?!) means "dubious move".

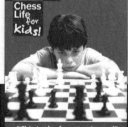

Part I
Focus on Openings

Game 1:Tal is Smiling

Those who like to attack and who believe that "tempo is gold" will enjoy, and greatly benefit from, the writings and games of their "patron saint", Mikhail Tal.

Our contributor, Michael Coon (the namesake of the 8th World Champion, Mikhail being the Russian spelling of the great Archangel's name) knew little of Smith-Morra theory when he employed this gambit on a friend's advice. But Michael's instincts were just fine.

Writes Mr. Coon:
I am 54 years old. This tourney was held in Ann Arbor, Michigan, on September 7, 2008. My ranking was 1418 on the label of the September *Chess Life* magazine. My opponent was Michael Dang, rated 1588.

This was the third round game. We were each 1-1.

Sicilian Defense
Smith-Morra Gambit [B21]
Michael Coon (1418)
Michael Dang (1588)
Ann Arbor, MI, 9/2008

1. e4 c5
The Sicilian again. My first round opponent, a 1612, had soundly thrashed me when my attack failed. But I was determined to play better this time.
2. d4 cxd4 3. c3 dxc3 4. Nxc3

I played a gambit suggested by a friend of mine who said it fit my attacking style.
For his pawn, White got several tempos — a knight on c3, open lines for the queen and both bishops. The theory views this position as equal — White has compensation for a pawn, but not more.
4. ... d6 5. Bc4 Nc6 6. Nf3 Nf6

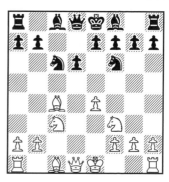

7. 0-0
So far, so good. I castled at this

point so my attack could not be ruined later on by a surprise check that would bail out my opponent. Also this would eventually enable me to develop my rook to e1 where it could be useful in controlling the center.

Black's sixth move is viewed as inaccurate, as it allows 7. e5!, with some advantage for White (see Game 3). Black, of course, shouldn't lose a queen after 7. ... Nxe5? 8. Nxe5 dxe5 9. Bxf7+; but even stronger moves like 7. ... dxe5 8. Qxd8+! Nxd8! (8. ... Kxd8? 9. Ng5!) and 7. ... Ng4 8. exd6. Mr. Coon, not knowing the theory, follows opening principles (early castle) — the right strategy under such circumstances!

7. ... g6 8. Ng5

Here I jumped on the opportunity to start to attack.

After 7. ... g6 (safer was 7. ... e6, transferring to "normalcy") 8. e5 gains even more in strength, compared to 7. e5 (as in my earlier comment).

8. ... Ne5 9. Qb3

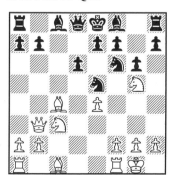

Protecting the bishop and bringing another piece to bear on his f7 pawn.

9. ... Nxc4

The only defense was 9. ... e6.

10. Qxc4

He traded pieces but the threat is still there.

Two threats — and there is no way to stop both.

10. ... e6

He shut the door on that threat but ...

Relatively better was 10. ... Be6.

11. Nb5

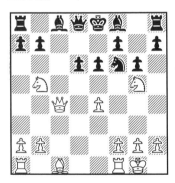

When in doubt, castle!

Comments in italics within games belong to Lev Alburt.

The other knight rides into battle, threatening the rook and king fork. I did not see a way for him to counter this and was sure I would at least win the Exchange. *Black could try 11. ... Rb8, but White's position will be overwhelming after either 12. Be3 (eyeing the a7-square and thus the rook) or 12. Rd1.*

11. ... d5

A queen threat will usually put a temporary halt to things while the queen is moved to safety.

Black's counterattack required White to play accurately, and boldly — and White did.

12. Nc7+

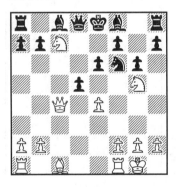

The knight's quest was not going to be delayed; besides, I wanted his king stuck in the center where I could easily get at him.

Excellent!

12. ... Ke7

If 12. ... Kd7, White had a pleasant choice between 13. exd5 and 13. Qb5+ Kxc7 14. Bf4+ (or first 14. Nxf7).

13. exd5

I considered checking the king again, but after he moves it, my queen is endangered again and I lose a tempo. If you are an attacker like me, sometimes a tempo is worth more than a minor piece and certainly more than a pawn.

The moves 13. Qc5+ Kd7 14. Qb5+ transfer into my comment to Black's 12th move (White wins). But 13. exd5 is equally strong.

13. ... Nxd5 14. Nxa8

Mission accomplished.

Well done!

14. ... Bd7

15. Bf4

I wanted to send the message "take the knight now or risk losing your chance forever."

Also winning is 15. Qc5+ and 16. Qxa7.

15. ... Qxa8

The temptation was too great. Now I have his queen virtually out of the game at a8. This should give me a couple of moves to operate before she can return to the action. Tempo is gold.

16. Rfe1

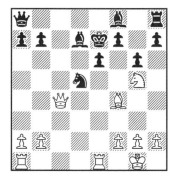

16. ... Nxf4 17. Qxf4

The attack has returned to f7, and the king's rook on e1 is sure to come in handy later.

17. ... Qe8

Now the mighty queen is tied down to a lowly pawn and still is of no use as an offensive threat.

18. Rad1

Grabbing the open file, threatening the bishop, and cutting off the king's later retreat.

18. ... Bc6

Tempo is gold

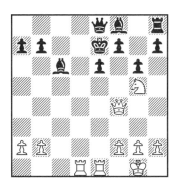

Hoping to somehow untangle his pieces.

19. Ne4

Threatening mate with the queen by covering the king's escape route and freeing the white queen for action.

Good move — but 19. Qd6+ Kf6 20. Qe5+ Ke7 21. Qxe6+! wins even faster.

After 21. Qxe6+!

19. ... Bxe4 20. Rxe4

Well, there goes another mate threat. But if I can double my rooks on the d-file, I can still cause some mischief.

White is ahead in material (an Exchange for a pawn) in addition to the black king's being stuck in the center. Not surprisingly, White is winning.

20. ... Qc6 21. Red4

The rooks are doubled up and it's three against one. The black queen, finally out of her hole, is alone against the white queen and two rooks. The black rook and bishop are still in the starting blocks.

21. ... f5

22. Qg5+

The lights are starting to flicker as the black king fights for his life.

The final assault is coming.

22. ... Kf7 23. Rd7+ Kg8

King to e8 would have been the end.

Yes, after 24. Qd8, checkmate.

24. Qf6

Now Qf7 is mate.

24. ... Qxd7 25. Rxd7 Be7

Delaying the inevitable.

26. Rxe7 h5 27. Qg7, mate.

Game 2: Setting Up An Attack

It's easier to attack than to defend.

Our contributor, Felix Chen, submitted an exciting game in which he emerges from a Smith-Morra Gambit with the opportunity to make a winning piece sacrifice.

My name is Felix Chen, and I live in San Jose, California. I am 14 years old, and I have a USCF rating of 1244. Here is a game that I think you will be interested in because of a surprising knight sacrifice on Move 23. It completely threw my opponent off guard, and I was able to have a huge attack on his exposed king.

This game was played at my local chess club on Thursday evening, March 2. My opponent was a young man named Bill Halphin, a USCF 1200-rated player. So we were sort of equal. I really hope you enjoy this game.

Sicilian Defense,
Smith-Morra Gambit [B21]
Felix Chen (1244)
Bill Halphin (1200)
Kolty Chess Club, 2005

1. e4 c5 2. d4 cxd4 3. c3 dxc3
4. Nxc3 e6

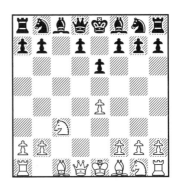

After my opponent played this move, the game was out of the opening book, so I had to be on the lookout for tactical errors.

Well, this is a more or less standard Smith-Morra position.

5. Nf3 a6 6. Bc4 b5 7. Bb3

Here, I think that White is better because of the piece activity. None of Black's pieces are developed, while White has three pieces already active. Some may argue that piece activity is not enough compensation for the sacrificed pawn, but I think it is sufficient enough.

7. ... Bb4

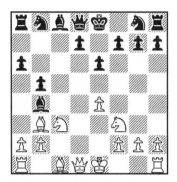

This move seems to be out of place. Even though it develops a piece and pins the white queen's knight on c3, that is easily taken care of by 8. 0-0. Now, after 8. 0-0, the bishop is useless on that square, and my opponent either has to retreat later on, or give up the bishop pair. Plus, knights should usually be developed before bishops.

8. 0-0

Stronger was 8. Qd4 — the idea Felix noted later, in his comments to 9. Qe2.

8. ... Ne7

I think the reason why my opponent played this instead of 8. ... Nf6 was because he was afraid of 9. e5. I'm not so sure.

If so, he was right: 8. ... Nf6 9. e5 clearly favors White.

9. Qe2

I missed a better move here. 9. Qd4 is superior because it forks the bishop on b4 and the g7 pawn. I was moving too quickly, and didn't see this. Usually, I play Qe2 because the queen goes

to that square in the Morra Gambit, followed by the rook lining up against the enemy queen and the bishop later on the same diagonal as the black queen.

Moral: don't play (and think) by rote. When your opponent deviates from a book line, try to take advantage of it.

9. ... 0-0 10. Rd1 Nbc6

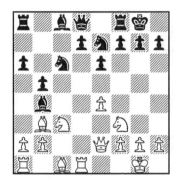

11. Bf4

Stronger is 11. e5!, freeing both the e4-square and the b1-h7 diagonal.

11. ... Ng6 12. Bg3

Here, I wanted to keep my nice diagonal slicing into his exposed queenside in case Mr. Halpin decided to move his queen off the "d" file my rook was on.

12. ... Bxc3

I was pretty happy about this move because he traded his good bishop for my bad knight. My c3 knight had little mobility since his pawns on a6 and b5 kept it locked in.

Correct. Better was 12. ... Na5, with approximate equality (White will have full compensation for a pawn, but not more).

13. bxc3 Na5

Mr. Halphin wants to get rid of my bishop pair here. I don't know if it was better to let him do it, or retreat, but you'll see what I did in a few moves.

14. Rac1

This was probably my worst move throughout this game. Even though it partially increases the rook's activity, I'm really not going to be pushing up my "c" pawn. I really don't have a clue what a better move would be right now. But I do know that 14. Rac1 was definitely not the greatest move.

The move isn't terrible and not even bad — but also hardly useful. Why not 14. h4! here? Still, White remains better.

14. ... Nxb3

Yep, a trade. Even though I don't have the two bishops any more, neither does my opponent. Since we have opposite color bishops, the side that is *attacking*

gets the better deal out of it. So you can naturally guess what my plan is here.

15. axb3 Qa5

My opponent finally decided to move his queen off the same file as my rook. But the square he went to is probably not the best one. Even so, Mr. Halphin is attempting to get his queen into the game somehow, and that tells me to start implementing my plan.

16. h4

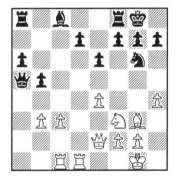

I don't know about you, GM Alburt, but I went over this game with my chess teacher, Albert Rich, and both of us agreed that this was a good move. It starts my assault on the black king, and threatens to kick out the defending knight next turn. It also ignores the fact that the enemy queen is trying to penetrate my queenside. In fact, I wanted the queen to stay there because it really has no purpose on a5. Although 16. h4 exposes my own king, Black does not have enough pieces in action to exploit this weakness.

An excellent point. 16. h4! is a great move! Remember a rule of thumb: when the opponent's knight is on g6 (or g3) play h2-h4-h5 (or ... h7-h5-h4).

16. ... f6

I don't think too highly of this move. Black's king is now more exposed, letting the attack begin.

17. h5

The black knight is forced to retreat and become passive.

17. ... Ne7

The only square that doesn't make the knight look stupid. This allows me to start ripping into his kingside.

18. Bd6

Threatens and pins the e7 knight. Black has two moves that protect the piece and unpin. My opponent chose

18. ... Re8 19. Nh4

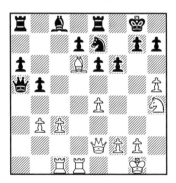

Mr. Rich and I thought that this move was great. The knight has a tighter grip on the light squares (it can't be exploited because the Black light-squared bishop is still

inactive) and my queen can now be introduced into the attack.

Yes, the move is great! And Felix is definitely correct regarding his queen.

19. ... Qb6

There is no threat in this move. My d1 rook protects my bishop on d6. I suppose that Mr. Halphin is trying to get more defenders over to the kingside This will take a while, so I proceed in my attack while he regroups.

20. h6

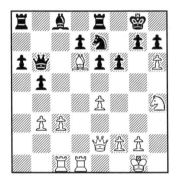

This pawn sacrifice required some time to calculate (I had an hour and fifteen minutes left, so I was in no hurry). Mr. Halphin cannot accept the pawn because after 20. ... gxh6, 21. Qh5 forks the pawn on h6 and the e8 rook.

After the rook moves, the knight on e7 is lost because its protector was forced to move. There is also the possibility of 21 . ... Kf8 instead of moving the rook. But, after 22. Qxh6+ Kg8 (22. ... Kf7 leads to checkmate), the king is sitting on a lift file, and 23. Rd3 prepares to access it.

The calculations are correct, but too deep (an overkill). Usually such a pawn can be sacrificed intuitively, trusting that something will be there. Certainly, it's how Tal played.

20. ... g6

Mr. Halphin probably saw the capture was not beneficial to him. But now, his kingside is weakening dramatically, and all that needs to be done is to bring in the main attacker. If he ignored the pawn and played another move, then 21. Qg4 threatens mate.

21. Qg4

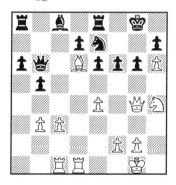

This move sets up a knight sacrifice on g6 that I saw after I played 20. h6. I was totally amazed after I calculated it out. If Mr. Halphin cooperated and didn't make an annoying move, then the effects would be devastating. I'm sure that you saw how awesome this combination was back at move 20!

I was happy when I saw his next move, and I'm sure you would have been, too, if you were playing in this position.

21. ... Bb7

There is no threat to this move, and it is a futile attempt to connect his rooks and give him more breathing space. Mr. Halphin thankfully did not expect to see my next moves that would result in an obvious lost game for him.

Yes, if Black had seen your threat, he would have played 21. ... Kf7. White's attack is very strong (e.g., after 22. Bxe7 Rxe7 23. e5). But he still has work to do.

After
23. e5!

22. Bxe7

Here I enter into the combination. This move is necessary for the sacrifice because it only works if the pawn on h7 takes on g6, and the other defender is the black knight. So I remove it.

22. ... Rxe7

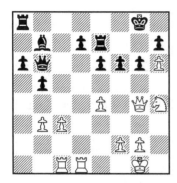

Mr. Halphin has to get his material back, or else it is a lost game for him.

23. Nxg6

This is the climactic point of the combination. If the sacrifice is accepted with 23. ... hxg6, 24. Qxg6+ trips through. If 24. ... Kf8, then 25. h7 forces Black to lose material. 24. ... Kh8 leads to the same thing. Black will not survive long after this.

23. ... hxg6

Black accepts, and a shocked Mr. Halphin sees the results of his miscalculation right before his eyes.

Not accepting will also lose, as quickly as accepting the knight.

24. Qxg6+ Kh8

It didn't matter which way Mr. Halphin went. Both ways lead to a loss in material for the black side.

25. Qxf6+

Forking Black's king and rook. This was the purpose of my sacrifice on g6. Mr. Halphin though that the sacrifice would not be sound, but he was definitely wrong.

Yes, the game is over.

25. ... Kh7

Attacks White's pawn on h6. Black gets a pawn, at least, for a rook.

26. Qxe7+

This is the obvious. A rook for a pawn is a decisive material advantage.

26. ... Kxh6

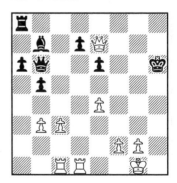

Mr. Halphin wins a pawn, but

this is definitely not enough for a rook.

27. Rxd7

I later realized that 27. Qf6+ leads to an unstoppable mate when I analyzed it with Mr. Rich. The game would have ended a bit earlier, but this is okay.

27. ... Bxe4

Mr. Halphin was in such a material deficit, that he seized all the material that was available. Unfortunately, he didn't stop to see what would happen after the materialistic capture.

28. Qh4+

Now, Black is in big trouble. This check forks Black's bishop and king.

28. ... Kg6

This was the only move for Black. Unfortunately, it leads to another devastating fork.

29. Qxe4+

This is just pitiful now. Black is about to lose a rook, which puts him at a ten-point material disadvantage. Mr. Halphin knew that it was pointless to continue two rooks down, so he resigned after this check.

Black resigns.

I was really impressed by the results of this sacrifice; when I first looked at it, I didn't think it would make a big difference if I executed it. Looking back at the results of this game, I now realize how wrong my first impression was.

This game is full of sacrifices. First, opening sacrifice — the Smith-Morra Gambit, achieving just enough compensation for a pawn. Then, a pawn sacrifice which Black, correctly, didn't accept (20. h6), followed by 23. Nxg6, a three-move-deep winning combination.

Game 3: A True Gambiteer Attack
And a winning defensive move overlooked by many.

Writes Mr. Bogin:
Enclosed is a game I played in the second round of the Vermont Resort Open. I think that it exemplifies the kind of gambit play required in dynamic positions such as those arising from the Smith-Morra gambit. My opponent followed a book line, deviating on Move 13 in an innovation that opened the position — undesirably for him, since his king was stranded in the center. I followed the techniques outlined in *The King in Jeopardy*, of further opening the center by any means possible and ultimately succeeded.

I'm very glad Theo was able to apply the above principle so well, and that **The King In Jeopardy** *was of real help!*

Sicilian Defense
Smith-Morra Gambit [B21]
Theo Bogin (1692)
Kurt English (1734)
Vermont Resort Tournament, 2005

1. e4 c5 2. d4 cxd4 3. c3
The Smith-Morra Gambit, which gives White lasting pres-

sure and piece activity in exchange for a pawn.
3. ... dxc3 4. Nxc3 Nc6 5. Nf3 d6 6. Bc4

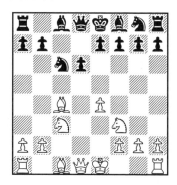

6. ... Nf6?
This move renders Black susceptible to the dangerous e5 attack, based on the c4 bishop and the once-defended queen on d8. The move 6. ... e6 seems safer, since it closes up the a2-g8 diagonal.
Technically speaking, the d8-queen is defended twice — but even this isn't enough here.
7. e5
Here my opponent thought for a while, and found a reasonable continuation that coincided with the book line up until Move 13.
7. ... Ng4
If 7. ... Nxe5??, then 8. Nxe5 dxe5 9. Bxf7+ Kxf7 10. Qxd8, winning the queen.
The other alternative was 7. ...

dxe5 which, after 8. Qxd8+

After 8. Qxd8+

8. ... Nxd8 (8. ... Kxd8 9. Ng5) 9. Nb5 Rb8 10. Nxe5 (threatening 11. ... Nc7 mate) 10. ... e6, leaves Black cramped and hamstrung and White with ample compensation for the pawn.

8. e6

Breaking up the pawns around Black's king and cutting off the c8-bishop from the defense of g4.

*Hannes Langrock (*The Modern Morra Gambit*) questions this move because of 8. ... fxe6 9. Ng5 Nge5!, and recommends the solid 8. exd6, with compensation.*

8. ... Bxe6 9. Bxe6 fxe6 10. Ng5!

Attacking the g4-knight while simultaneously hitting pawn on e6.

10. ... Nf6

11. 0-0

Best was the natural 11. Nxe6 Qd7 12. Qe2, and White has at least full compensation for a pawn.

11. ... Qd7 12. Re1

Hitting e6 a second time and forcing Black to open the a2-a8 diagonal.

12. ... e5 13. Qb3

Capitalizing on the weak a2-g8 diagonal, and threatening 14. Qf7+, after which the black king will be stranded in the center.

13. ... Nd4

The move 13. ... 0-0-0 loses to 14. Nf7, forking the two rooks.

The more passive 13. ... Nd8 (defending f7) loses to 14. f4 (prying open the center) 14. ... h6 15. fxe5 hxg5 16. exf6 gxf6

After 16. ... gxf6

17. Nd5 (light-square blockade, a la Nimzovich) 17. ... Rh6 18. Nxe7 Bxe7 19. Qg8 mate.

After the simple 13. ... d5, Black is much better — probably wining. Like so many of us, he overlooked this obvious defense. Perhaps we were all too trusting. Mr. Bogin trusted his book; Mr. English trusted his opponent; I trusted Mr. Bogin and his book. This chain of errors was broken by my editor, Al Lawrence, an Expert who, in less than a minute, pointed out 13. ... d5 to me.
14. Qf7+ Kd8 15. Be3!?

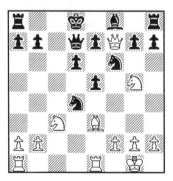

White wants the use of the e6-

square for his knight, and the d4-knight acts as guardian of this important central square.
15. ... h6?
An *intermezzo* that unfortunately drops a pawn.
16. Bxd4 hxg5 17. Bxe5 Kc7
Trying to flee with the king to the queenside. 17. ... dxe5?? loses to 18. Red1 Nd5 19. Rxd5, pinning and winning the black queen.
After 17. ... Qe8 White avoids the exchange of queens by 18. Qb3 and the bishop is untouchable. Perhaps 17. ... Rc8 was the best defense — no forced win, but White's attack still far outweighing a missing pawn.
18. Bxf6

Eliminating the final guardian of the light squares and preparing to plant a knight on the wonderful d5 square.
18. ... gxf6
The move 18. ... exf6?? loses prettily to 19. Nd5+ Kd8 (19. ... Kc6 20. Rac1+ wins the queen and 19. ... Kc8 loses to 20. Re8+)

20. Re8+ Qxe8 21. Qc7 mate.

After 21.Qc7 mate

19. Nd5+ Kd8 20. Nxf6!

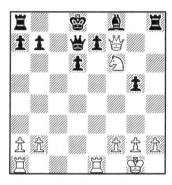

20. ... Qb5
The rook is lost with 20. ... gxf6 Qxf6+.
21. a4!
Beginning to rob the queen of all her squares on the critical a4-e8 diagonal.
*White employs a very important chess tool, **deflection***.
21. ... Qc6 22. Rec1, Black resigns.
He is going to lose his queen (queen's retreat allows 23. Qe8 mate.)

Game 4: The Expanding Center

Think long and hard when facing an early opening surprise — perhaps this "non-theoretical" move is a mistake which allows, and deserves, swift punishment. Resist the temptation to go quickly into familiar — and not so promising — lines.

I've picked up the game below not for its brilliancies, but for its very common (alas) errors. The first came already on move two as a provocative, and bad, 2. ... Nc6, and for two more moves Black allowed (invited!), and White refused to apply, the punishing d4-d5.

In the final stage of this short game, rich in both strategy and tactics, Black failed to find an adequate developing plan, thus permitting his opponent, Rob Dolan, to expose the black king to a decisive attack.

Writes Mr. Dolan:

This game was played in the San Diego Chess Club in Balboa Park; the time controls were G/40. I had performed fairly well in the previous rounds, having two wins and a draw against another Class A player. Now all that stood between me and first place was my opponent.

Sicilian Defense [B22]
Rob Dolan (1788)
Joselito Penaflor (1904)
San Diego Chess Club, 2008

1. e4 c5 2. d4 Nc6?!

My opponent declined the Smith-Morra Gambit. If he takes on d4 then I offer another pawn with 3. c3 and if he takes on c3 then I recapture with the knight, gaining rapid development for the price of a pawn and resulting in lots of pressure on the black position. When my opponent declined the gambit in this fashion, I knew he was not familiar with these ideas for White or Black and I instantly felt that I was going to get a big advantage.

*In my book, 2. ... Nc6 deserved a full question mark. Declining the Smith-Morra is fine, but it should be done in the right way. Black's two best choices are (after 2. ... cxd4 3. c3) the conventional 3. ... Nf6 or the more rare 3. ... g6 4. cxd4 d5! (a must!), the latter line described in detail in **Black Book**.*

3. c3

Here I should have played 3. d5! Which pushes the knight around while gaining space in the center, but since I normally play the c3 Sicilian (1. e4 c5 2. c3) I felt very comfortable going back into familiar lines. Also, if my opponent had captured on d4 with 3. ... cxd4 I simply recapture 4. cxd4 and I've got a nice two-pawn center on d4 and e4.

Unfortunately, Rob didn't act on his instant feeling (yes, 3. d5 gives White a real, substantive edge (after, for example, 3. ... Ne5 4. f4 Ng6 5. Nf3). And in the line he opted for, the move 4. ... d5 (after 3. ... cxd4 4. cxd4) takes care of White's nice center, while the only "familiar" line to be reached , with 5. exd5 Qxd5 6. Nf3, leads only to equality. Rob faced a clear choice — a large advantage or an apparent familiarity (and equality), and he made an archetypically (alas) wrong choice.

3. ... e6

As shown in my previous note,

3. ... cxd4 4. cxd4 d5! was both needed, and adequate, for achieving equality.

4. Nf3

White's best here is the same 4. d5, albeit his edge here (after 4. ... Ne5) is smaller than in the 3. d5 line. Remember: if you can push a central pawn to the fifth rank attacking the enemy knight, do it — or at least consider it very seriously.

4. ... Nf6

Better is 4. ... d5!.

5. d5!

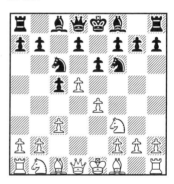

Now the central assault begins! Black's c6-knight is going to have to find a new home, while White is winning space, tempo, and awesome piece development.

5. ... exd5

A serious mistake. Black had to play either 5. ... Nb8 or the more provocative 5. ... Ne7. In both cases he's worse but by no more than +/=.

6. exd5 Nb8

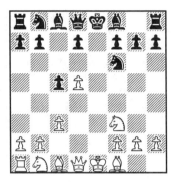
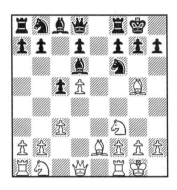

7. Bg5

If 7. d6! Qb6 8. Qe2+! Kd8 9. Ne5 Bxd6 10. Nxf7+, White wins the rook while permanently confining the black king to the center. I found that variation after the game, but my move, 7. Bg5, develops a new piece, pins the knight to the queen, and prevents the bishop from coming to e7 because of 8. d6. If he tries to check with the queen I simply develop my bishop to e2 and then castle. *If Black had nothing better than to lose a rook as given above, then undoubtedly, 7. d6 was an easy winner, while 7. Bg5 would have required a big question mark. However, after 7. d6 Ne4! 8. Qe2 f5 9. Nfd2, while White is winning, the game is not over yet.*

7. ... Bd6?

Perhaps 7. ... d6 was relatively better

8. Be2 0-0 9. 0-0

9. ... b6

My opponent's bishop on c8 is unable to develop on the c8-h3 diagonal because his dark square bishop is blocking his d7-pawn. Moving his pawn to b6, he tries to get the light-square bishop to either b7 or a6.

Black is severely cramped and finding it hard to develop! *Another critical moment in the game. To get out of the bind, Black has to play ... d7-d6 (the attempt to develop with 9. ... b6 is inadequate, as will be clear very soon). Thus I'd suggest 9. ... h6, and if 10. Bh4, then 10.... g5 11. Bg3 Bxg3 12. hxg3 d6; also deserving attention is 9. ... Re8, preparing ... Bf8 (and then ... d7-d6).*

10. c4 Na6 11. Nc3 Nc7

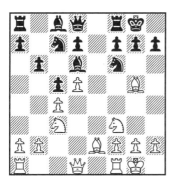

Black's last three moves were a pure waste of time.

12. Ne4

White is winning

12. ... Qe7

Now Black is dancing to my tune. I'm forcing him to defend for the rest of the game. If 12. ... Be7, 13. d6! wins a piece.

13. Bd3 h6

Poor Black is trying desperately to break the pin, but White no longer needs it and simplifies the position.

Too late indeed!

14. Nxf6+ gxf6 15. Bxh6 Re8

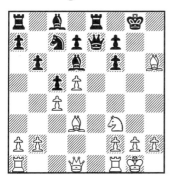

16. Re1?!

I missed the impressive 16. Nd4! which leads to quick victory no matter now Black responds.

True, but White still has many easy roads to victory.

16. ... Qd8 17. Ne5 Kh8?

I threaten mate if Black captures the knight. Now I could instantly win the queen with 18. Nxf7+ but I saw an even better move.

18. Qg4!, Black resigned

Black resigned, because there is no defense to mate. If Black playcd 18. ... Rg8, 19. Nxf7 mate, and capturing the knight allows 19. Qg7 mate.

I was beyond excited to have beaten such a high-rated player in this fashion, and as a result I took clear first in the under-1800 category, won $75, and achieved a class A rating. It will be a very memorable game and tournament for the rest of my chess career.

More On The d4-d5 Charge

In the Alekhine Defense, a d4-d5 pawn thrust attacking the c6-knight usually leads to White's advantage.

In the game below Black, trying to avoid theoretical disputes, early played ... Nc6 — refutable by d5. White, however, for several moves refused to push his queen pawn.

**Alekhine's Defense,
Exchange Variation [B03]**
Ted Doykos (1825)
Derek Fish (1649)
5th Annual Al Ufer Memorial

1. e4 Nf6 2. e5 Nd5 3. d4 d6 4. c4 Nb6 5. exd6 cxd6 6. Nc3 Nc6

Right off the bat, I see I have a well-prepared opponent. After six months of chess starvation in college, I wasn't up to any theoretical disputes, so I avoided the main line, 6. ... g6.

Black chooses the wrong way to avoid the theory. He plays a sharp line — an asymmetrical 5. ... cxd6 — and then plays a dubious 6. ... Nc6, punishable by 7. d5, with a clear edge (Mr. Fish himself notes this in his next comment). To avoid sharp theory-is-a-must lines, Mr. Fish should have played the symmetrical, simple 5. ... exd6, where little concrete knowledge is required.

7. Be3 g6
Ted overlooks the straightforward 7. d5 Ne5 8. Be2 (the c4 pawn is immune thanks to the threat of Qa4+), and I overlook the straightforward 7. ... d5 8. c5 Nc4, with a familiar Alekhine position. At a certain point in chess development, we can forget that sometimes the straightforward moves are the best moves.

Straightforward moves are usually the best, However, the line 7. ... d5 8. c5 Nc4 9. Bxc4 dxc4 10. Qa4 Be6 11. Rd1 favors White.

8. Rc1 Bg7 9. b3
My knights are clearly making Ted nervous, so he takes a move off to try to isolate them, despite the obvious strength of the d4-d5 advance. Meanwhile, he's falling behind in development and three turns away from castling.

9. ... 0-0

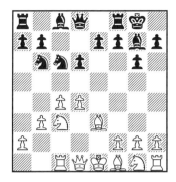

Via transpositions (and mutual errors — missing d4-d5!) a true theoretical position is reached. The right move — of course, 10. d5! — will advantage White.

10. Be2 e5

I probably should have block-aded the d4 pawn, but I completely missed the strange-looking 10. ... d5 11. c5 Nd7 12. Nxd5 Ndb8 (the knight gets lost and ends up in the wrong stable!) and I get the pawn back.

I like this line! (But 10. ... e5 is also OK).

11. dxe5

Now with Black's pawn on e5 — rather than on e7 — 11. d5 is playable, but not that strong; 11. dxe5 is to be preferred.

11. ... dxe5

(After several ups and downs, White blundered a piece and lost)

Game 5: Lost On Move Four — And Then Winning

Chess principles are stated over and over for a good reason — they can provide a shortcut to finding good moves. But make sure there is in fact a principle before you follow it.

In Topalov-Kramnik (the second game of their match) Black allowed mate in three — and Topalov missed it, too! Perhaps Topalov, subconsciously or not, trusted his opponent. Later missing another, albeit not so simple, win, White eventually blundered one more time and lost.

A similar scenario happened in the next game. Donald Padgett, playing Black, plays a novelty on Move 4, allowing his opponent, a Master, to win a piece for just a pawn. White missed this opportunity, and then, on the next move, missed another opportunity, this time to win a pawn. Interestingly, Donald — who won the game and submitted otherwise quite good comments — didn't mention these mutual blunders.

Writes Donald:

This game underscores the following principles:

In general, when given a choice between taking back with a more valuable or less valuable piece, take back with the less valuable piece.

(I doubt there is such a rule. It all depends on concrete cir- cumstances — LA).

Avoid the mistake of driving your opponent's pieces to better squares.

The chess adage "A knight on the rim is grim" is not always true.

Alekhine's Defense [B04]
Alexander Chua (2280)
Donald Padgett (1780)
Dallas CC Swiss

1. e4 Nf6
I like the Alekhine Defense because it encourages White to move the same pawn twice in the opening. While Black is letting White build a pawn center, Black can mount a fierce counterattack. Plus, knight moves can be taken back, but pawn moves are permanent.

2. e5 Nd5
White pushes the pawn to chase the knight and gain more space.

3. d4 d6
The counterattack begins ...

4. Nf3 b6

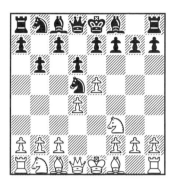

White develops the king knight and protects the e5 pawn. Black moves the b pawn to prepare an attack on the base of the pawn chain at d4.

I thought I had tried every possible move here: 4. ... Bg4, 4. ... g6, 4. ... c6, 4. ... dxe5, 4. ... Nc6, even 4. ... Nb6. Well, it's OK to look for new moves and ideas — but such moves should be carefully checked. Here, both opponents missed 5. c4 Nb4 6. Qa4+ winning a piece: 6. ... N4c6 7. d5; 6. ... N8c6 7. a3.

5. a3 c5

White is thinking of trying to trap the black knight, but the c-pawn advance creates an escape square and attacks the base of White's central pawn pair.

6. Bc4

Rather than simply develop his pieces, White should have looked for ways to exploit the weakness of his opponent's light squares: 6. dxc5, winning a pawn (if 6. ... dxc5?, 7. Bb5+).

6. ... Bb7

White develops his king's bishop to attack the unprotected black knight on d5. Black develops the queen bishop to protect the knight.

7. 0-0 e6

White castles while Black over-protects his centrally posted d5 knight with the e-pawn.

8. Re1 Be7

White puts his rook opposite the black king and protects the e5 pawn a second time. Black prepares to castle and guards the g5 square from the white knight.

9. exd6 Bxd6

White exchanges pawns to try to open up the center against the uncastled black king.

10. Nbd2 0-0

White develops the queen knight and Black castles kingside.

11. Ne4 Be7

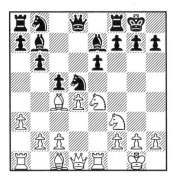

White attacks the bishop causing the bishop to move to the useful e7 square, which guards the d8-h4 diagonal from the knights on e4 and f3.

White's tactical misses on Moves 5 and 6 and his uninspired play thereafter allowed Black to achieve a practically equal game. Now White has to work very hard to achieve even the smallest edge. My favorite candidate moves are 12. Bg5 and 12. Bb3 (the latter planning to dislodge Black's centralized knight).

12. dxc5 bxc5

White trades the center d4 pawn for the black c5 pawn — perhaps hoping to trade his knight for the dark square bishop or create an isolated pawn on c5. I follow the principle of taking back with the less valuable piece and move the pawn towards the center. Plus, the isolani pawn prevents the white f3 knight from being able to move to central d4 square.

13. b3 Nbd7 14. Bb2 N7f6

I don't like the white bishop aimed at my g7 pawn, so I block it with the d7 knight as well as getting the knight to a more active square.

15. Ng3 Qc7

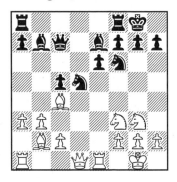

White avoids trading pieces to keep the game more tactical. Black gets the queen off the back rank, protects the c5 pawn a second time, and takes aim at the white kingside.

16. Qd2

Loses a tempo. To stop ... Nf4, why not 16. Be5, with a good game?

16. ... Rad8

White makes a similar developing move by moving the queen to the second rank. Black follows the positional concept of putting a rook opposite the queen.

17. Qe2 Nf4!

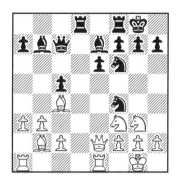

White moves to get away from opposite the discovered attack from the rook, but enables the knight to move with a threat and gain of tempo against White.

18. Qf1 Nh3+!

White moves the queen next to the king to increase king safety. However, that safety is illusory. The black knight check on h3 looks counterintuitive because the g2 pawn protects h3 and the chess adage "a knight on the rim is grim." However, the black knight on h3 overloads the g2 pawn, because the g2 pawn must also protect the f3 knight. If White's g-pawn takes the knight, the black bishop takes the now unprotected white f3 knight, which leaves White with an exposed kingside pawn structure and doubled pawns on the h-file.

19. Kh1 Ng4!

White tries to avoid a shattered kingside pawn structure, but Black brings in the second knight to attack the f2 pawn twice, which is only guarded by

the white queen once.
Knight moves deserve their exclams.

20. gxh3 Bxf3+

White gets saddled with double h-pawns and an exposed kingside. Black takes back with check to gain another tempo.

21. Kg1

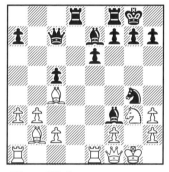

21. ... Nh6

Again I move the knight to the rim, because I do not want to block the f-pawn. Also, I like the idea of being able to move the knight from h6 to f5.

Excellent!

22. Re3 Bb7

White tries to eradicate the menacing black bishop, which I move out of harm's way to b7. Notice the white king has no safe squares.

23. Rae1

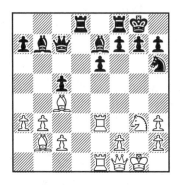

23. ... Bd6
White doubles the rooks on the e-file, and Black creates a battery spearheaded by the black bishop on the b8-h2 diagonal. Notice the white g3 knight is in an absolute pin, for if it moves, the black bishop renders mate at h2.

24. Bd3 Nf5
White aims his white bishop at the black kingside, but now the black knight threatens both the e3 rook and pinned black knight on g3.

25. Bxf5 exf5

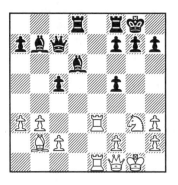

White is forced to exchange

his light square bishop for the knight. Notice that White still cannot take the unprotected f5 pawn because of the absolute pin on the g3 knight by the queen/bishop battery.

26. Be5 f4!
White tries to exchange the dark square bishops to take the momentum out of Black's attack, but Black makes an in-between move (zwischenzug) by pushing the pawn to f4 — attacking the knight and rook a second time.

27. Bxd6 Rxd6
White exchanges bishops and Black develops the d8-rook to the d6 rank. Once again, I followed the principle of taking back with the less valuable piece.

Here, 27. ... Rxd6 is winning, but it has nothing to do with the non-existent principle of "taking back with the less valuable piece." In fact, 27. ... Qxd6 also wins easily.

28. Re7 Qc6!
White makes the natural move of the rook to the seventh rank, but only causes the black queen to move to the more useful c6 square, forming a battery spearheaded by the queen glaring down the exposed a8-h1 diagonal.

29. Ne4 Rg6+!
White blocks the a8-h1 diagonal, moves the knight away from capture, and threatens the black d6-rook. However it chases away the rook to the menacing g6

square with check and another gain in tempo.

30. Kh1 f5!

The white king is forced to the corner, putting the e4-knight into a crippling pin. Black immediately exploits this with f5 — attacking the pinned knight again.

31. Qc4+ Kh8

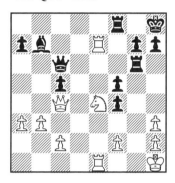

32. Rf7!? Rxf7!

White is following the principle that the best defense is a good offense, so he mounts a counter-attack by threatening back rank checkmate. However, Black takes back to deflect the white queen away from the vulnerable e4 knight.

Well done.

33. Qxf7 Qe4+!

Black sacks the queen with an exchange sacrifice and a forcing combination that culminates in checkmate.

34. Rxe4 Bxe4+ 35. f3 Bxf3, mate.

A dramatic upset, and an exciting game.

Game 6: Queen to King's Rook Five, Check(mate)!

Of course, games like 1. g4 e6 2. f4 Qh4 checkmate are extremely rare. However, Qh5 (or ... Qh4) checks are frequent, and often truly consequential.

Sometimes very bad moves provide very instructive examples. Consider, for instance, **1. e4 e5 2. Nf3 f6?**. Black's second move is bad on many counts: it takes from the black king's knight its best square; it doesn't develop; and it makes castling problematic (after White's 3. Bc4).

Not surprisingly, normal moves like 3. d4 and 3. Bc4 give White a real edge. But 2. ... f6 has an additional drawback: it exposes the king on that vital h5-e8 diagonal, thus allowing **3. Nxe5!.**

After
3. Nxe5!

After 3. ... fxe5 4. Qh5+

After 4. ...
Qh5+

the normal defense, 4. ... g6, loses material to 5. Qe5+ Qe7 6. Qxh8 and now an attempt to catch the queen: 6. ... Nf6 7. d3,

as well as 6. ... Qxe4+ 7. Kd1 leaves White with a big, even decisive, edge. Which leaves **4. ... Ke7 5. Qxe5+ Kf7 6. Bc4+**.

After
6. Bc4+

Now 6. ... Kg6 loses quickly to 7. Qf5+ Kh6 8. d4+ g5 9. h4. Black's best is **6. ... d5 7. Bxd5+ Kg6,** controlling the f5-square with the bishop. White now has three pawns for a piece, and a wandering Black king as a target. **When calculating 3. Nxe5 on Move 3, there was no need to look any further!**

Now, however, let's find the best plan, and the best move. **8. h4!** threatening 9. h5+. If **8. ... h5, 9. Bxb7!** deflecting the defender of the f5-square (the same blow follows 8. ... h6). **9. ... Bd6,**

After
9. ... Bd6

and now the most precise is **10. Qa5**, to meet **10. ... Bxb7** with **11. Qf5+ Kh6 12. d4+**, winning (12. ... g5 13. Bxg5+).

Going back to the first diagram, Black's best is **3. ... Qe7** (not 3. ... d5? 4. Qh5+ g6 5. Nxg6. Another "trick" to remember) **4. Nf3 Qxe4+**

After 4. ... Qxe4+

and now, of course, **5. Be2**, planning to exploit the e-file with the black king and queen on it to gain even more developing tempi (Remember: if your king is safer than your opponent's — don't exchange queens!)

But Preston Herrington did not know this Qh5 check idea very well and thus didn't recognize the opportunity when it occurred. Writes Mr. Herrington:

───────────

This was a blitz internet game. My blitz rating on that internet site was 1231, and my opponent was rated 2123. I figured I would see how long I lasted. The game was over quickly, but not without some surprises.

───────────

Englund Gambit [A40]
Preston Herrington (1231)
Anonymous (2123)
Internet Blitz

1. d4
My standard opening move. Especially against someone rated 900 points higher, I thought I would stick with the familiar.
1. ... e5
This gambit can't be good for Black against top players, but it seems to sacrifice a pawn in order to change from a typical "queen pawn" opening (more positional) to a "king pawn" opening (full of attacking possibilities)
2. dxe5
Taking the pawn seems best.
2. ... Nc6
Developing and attacking the pawn. I am already aware that he will ultimately win the pawn back.
Not necessarily — see my comment to Black's next move.
3. Nf3
Developing and defending the pawn. When in doubt, it seems that Nf3 is almost always a sound move.

3. ... f6
Attacking the pawn again. This move seems risky, making the black kingside more vulnerable than necessary. Fritz 9 suggests 3. ... Qe7.

The theory goes 4. Qd5 f6 5. exf6 Nxf6,

After 5.
... Nxf6

with only partial compensation for a pawn.
4. e4

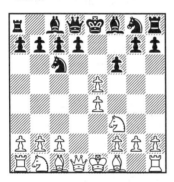

Here I chose development over the hopeless prospect of saving my pawn.

A reasonable decision in an unknown position — but why not take a look into ECO after the game is over? White's best is to play 4. exf6, with advantage.
4. ... Bc5
Black likewise develops

rather than capturing the pawn.
Black should play here 4. ... fxe5, e.g., 5. Bc4 Nf6 6. Nc3 Bc5, unclear (ECO).
5. Bc4
I considered 5. exf6, but now that we have a "kings pawn" opening, I wanted to develop as rapidly as possible, eager to castle.

Here not taking the pawn is the best, but for a different reason than simple castling: White now has higher goals.
5. ... Nxe5?

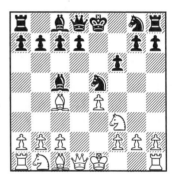

A big blunder, but I failed to take advantage. I'm afraid I had already fallen into the mindset that the huge rating difference meant my opponent wouldn't blunder.

Also bad now is 5. ... fxe5 as 6. Bxg8 Rxg8 7. Qd5 wins a piece.
6. Bb3
Perhaps still in the "queen pawn opening" mindset, I liked my bishop on this diagonal, but I was nervous that it was un-

guarded. I wanted to avoid 6. ...
Nxc4. I missed 6. Nxe5!! since 6.
... fxe5? allows 7. Qh5+!, winning material. Also very good
was 6. Bxg8! Rxg8 setting up the
fork 7. Qd5! where Black's best
hope is 7. ... Bxf2+. 6. Bxg8 was
completely counter to my strategic thinking:
(1) Bishops are better than
knights in open positions.
(2) My bishop is more developed than his knight.
(3) My bishop is preventing
... 0-0.
I missed winning tactics while
focusing on strategy, since I as-
sumed a much higher player
wouldn't blunder.
*Everybody can blunder, espe-
cially in blitz. Strategic thinking
should be brought in only after
tactical opportunities have been
examined.*
6. ... g6?!
This still leaves me the option
of 7. Bxg8!, since his bishop on
c5 is unprotected. Better for
Black was 6. ... d6. 6. ... g6 also
seems to make the kingside
rather "airy."
7. 0-0
Again, safe development did-
n't hurt me, but I missed 7. Bxg8!
7. ... d6
Perhaps he saw the need to
defend the bishop.
8. Nc3

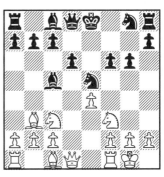

Continuing my development.
8. ... Bg4
Likewise developing. I was
worried after this move since my
f3 knight was pinned and I knew
that I would be forced to weaken
my kingside pawn structure with
gxf3 if and when Black chose to
capture my knight.
*It was better to worry before
"continuing development."
White could play, for instance, 8.
Nd4. But, as we'll see, this pin
isn't dangerous.*
9. Ba4+?
I'm afraid I panicked here,
hoping for Black to retreat the
bishop from g4. I could have
seized the initiative with 9. Bxg8!
Rxg8 10. Qd5 (forking the rook
and the b-pawn) 10. ... Rf8. Next
my knight could escape the pin
with 11. Nxe5.
*Of course, 9. Ba4+ is an in-
excusable loss of two (!) tempos.
Interestingly, besides the "normal" 9. Bxg8!, White also could
play 9. Nxe5 Bxd1 10. Nf7 and
here Black's best would be to recognize that preserving the queen*

is too risky and to return it with 10. ... Qe7 11 Rxd1 Qxf7!.

9. ... c6

The right move. Fritz now says the position is almost even, but in the game it felt like I was losing.

10. Bb3

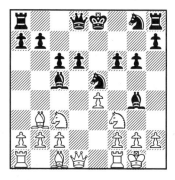

Getting the bishop back on the a2-g8 diagonal.

10. ... Qd7?!

Again my opponent gave an opportunity to take the initiative with 11. Nxe5, since 11. ... Bxd1? will lose a piece after 12. Nxd7 Kxd7 13. Rxd1.

Correct. Thus, Black should have executed his plan with an accurate 10. ... Qc8 — aiming to go to h3 while avoiding 11. Nxe5.

11. Be3?

Developing and hoping to simplify and distract Black from his attack on my kingside. Best was 11. Nxe5! (see above), but other moves that kept me alive were 11. Bf4 or 11. Kh1, anticipating the position after ...Bxf3.

Correct.

11. ... Bxf3 12. gxf3 Qh3!

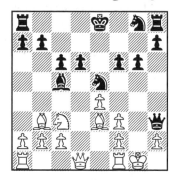

Doubling up on f3 with mating threats on h2.

13. Be6?

My bishop has to be on f4 to guard h2. So either 13. Bf4 or 13. Kh1 Nxf3 14. Bf4 was called for. Even better would have been to foresee this on Move 11 and play Bf4 then.

13. Bf4 (or 13. Kh1) would keep the game going — White is a pawn down, but not yet lost.

13. ... Nxf3+!!

I resigned, realizing I would have to give up my queen to avoid mate on h2.

Tactics reigned supreme in this game: first, missing Qh5+; second, missing (after the in-between Bxg8) the double-attack Qd5; then both ignoring and overreacting to the pin (8. ... Bg4); (Black) allowing — and (White) overlooking — 11. Nxe5; and finally, allowing the checkmate. A rich field for studying tactics!

Game 7: Opening Deviations, Or Crime and Punishment

First, a letter from Ryan Newhouse.

King's Indian Defense (E90)
Black: Ryan Newhouse
White: Nick Doulas
Turkey Open, 2003

**1. d4 Nf6 2. c4 g6 3. Nc3 Bg7
4. e4 d6 5. Nf3 Nbd7**

This move confused me. Black blocks his bishop, and the knight on d7 is limited. The text move is 5. ... 0-0.

---

*What should we do when our opponent surprises us on move five? Stop and think. There is a handy rule of thumb: **Assuming three minutes/move, (say 30/90) time control, on your first "crucial" move you should spend, on the average, half of the time you've saved on the earlier "book" moves, plus your stan-*

dard three minutes. For instance, if these first five moves took White one minute to make: $(5 \times 3-1):2=7 +3$ equals ten minutes.

Now, what to think about? The problem — if any — with the non-book 5. ... Nbd7 isn't strategic. The square d7 is often quite good for Black's queen knight in the King's Indian, and after the planned ... e7-e5 this knight will soon be ready to move (say, to c5 after d4-d5) and thus unblock his bishop. No, the only possible drawback of playing 5. ... Nbd7 before castling is tactical. After 6. e5 Black's f6-knight has no good places to go except the shaky g4.

However, having an opportunity to do something doesn't mean that you need to do it. For instance, if Black played 4. ... 0-0 instead of the more standard 4. ... d6, White could have played 5. e5, driving the black knight to e8. However, as Bobby Fischer has demonstrated, this early thrust leads only to equality; thus nowadays most players skip this dubious opportunity in favor of "normal" lines.

But even when your opponent's deviation from main line merits punishment, its degree varies. In the diagrammed position, after 6. e5! dxe5 7. dxe5

Ng4 8. e6 fxe6 9. Ng5

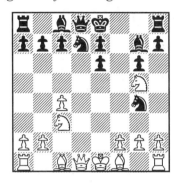

9. ... Nde5 10. Qxd8+ Kxd8 11. Bf4

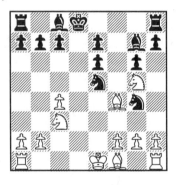

White achieves, according to ECO (always look into ECO after a game) a small edge. Thus Ryan had a choice: to analyze for 7-10 minutes the above lines, saying to himself: "I guess I should be better here; at least, I will not be worse." — and to play 6. e5. Or, after 3-5 minutes of analysis: "It looks too murky. I don't like it. Let me play what I always play against the King's Indian (in case Black plays the standard 5. ... 0-0), and be content with a 'nor-

mal' opening edge."

The actual game continued **6. Bd3** *(a reasonable move, employed by some GMs), and after some upheavals, Ryan eventually won.*

Young Alec Getz also missed an opportunity to punish his opponent for choosing a wrong move sequel in the opening. Alec writes: "I was nervous, so I decided to play aggressively instead of my usual defensive style."

Caro-Kann [B10]
Alec Getz
Igor Ummel
National Elementary, 2002

1. e4 c6 2. Nc3 d5 3. Nf3 dxe4
The most popular reply here is 3. ... Bg4.
4. Nxe4 Bf5
ECO recommends 4. ... Nf6 or (trying to transpose to "normalcy") 4. ... Nd7.
5. Ng3 Bg6

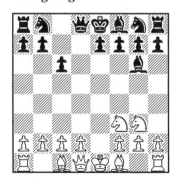

A blunder. This retreat is cor-

rect in the main line (2. d4 d5 3.
Nc3 dxe4 Nxe4 Bf5 5. Ng3 Bg6),

After
5. ...
Bg6

but not in the text, with the white
knight already on f3.
6. h4 h6 7. Ne5! Bh7

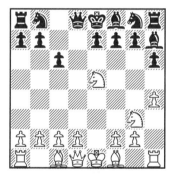

8. Bc4
Alex, perhaps playing too
fast, missed a golden opportunity.
The thrust 8. Qh5 forces Black to
play an ugly 8. ... g6 (8. ... Qd5?
9. Bc4!, winning) 9. Bc4 e6 10.
Qe2 with a big edge.
8. ... e6 9. Qf3
Here I had a good chance for
an attac**k.**
Not really — it was on move
eight.
9. ... Nf6 10. d3?

10. ... Nbd7?
It's even worse than Alec
thought. Black could have won a
knight by 10. ... Qa5+.
11. Nxd7 Qxd7
A pawn is saved by 11. ...
Nxd7, but Black clearly didn't see
what's coming.
12. Bxh6 *(! — LA)*

The first tactic! After 12. ...
gxh6 13. Qxf6, winning a pawn.
Alas, not the first.
12. ... gxh6 13. Qxf6 Rg8 14.
Nh5?

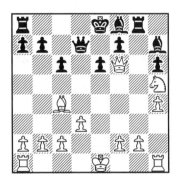

Looks like another hasty move. The situation has just changed sharply — White won a pawn, thus it was time to think (long), to plan, and to double-check your analysis! Here I realized that Black could now play 14. ... Bg6 and after, for instance, 15. Nf4 15. ... Bg7, win the queen. And if 15. Qf3 Bxh5 16. Qxh5 Rxg2 and Black is better. *(I'd say, rather, equal/unclear. — LA)* Luckily, my opponent did not play 14. ... Bg6.

14. ... Rg6?? 15. Qxg6 Bxg6 16. Nf6+!

The second tactic, winning the Exchange!

16. ... Kd8 17. Nxd7 Kxd7 18. h5 Bh7

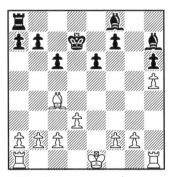

19. g4

White is up an exchange and a pawn — and thus is winning. Still, why put your pawns on your own bishop's color? White should have castled long, then played d4 and Bd3, exchanging light-square bishops. (No more bishop pair for Black).

19. ... a5 20. a4

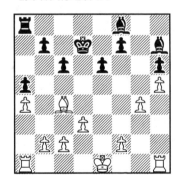

20. ...Bg7

The kingside dark squares would come under control after 20. ... Bd6!

21. c3 Rb8 22. Ke2 b5 23. axb5 cxb5 24. Bb3 a4 25. Bc2 e5 26. b3 axb3 27. Bxb3

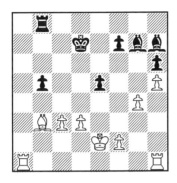

27. ... f5?? 28. Ra7+, Black resigns.
Winning both bishops! If 28.

Kc6 29. Rxg7 Rb7 30. Bd5+! Kxd5 31. Rxb7. If 28. ... Kc8 29. Be6+ Kd8 30. Rxg7 and Black cannot save his other bishop.

Perhaps Alec should adjust his style toward being more aggressive; it usually works! (It certainly worked for Alec in the above game). Also remember where to think longer — in those proverbial critical moments!

(Alex Getz since has become a strong Master, and a chess writer, too — not a surprise to me!)

Part II
Traps!

Game 8: Legal's Mate and Other Opening Traps

We all, from beginners to world champions, like to set up traps and especially opening traps (why not win as soon as possible?). In fact, a beginner who knows how to set up traps is no longer a true beginner, as he is becoming capable of planning ahead and anticipating opponent's possible reactions. Of course, not all traps are of equal value. Take, for instance, the position after 1. e4 e5 2. Nf3 Nc6 3. Bc4 d6 4. Nc3 Bg4

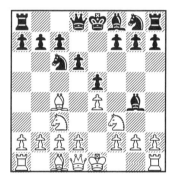

White can play 5. Nxe5, hoping for 5. ... Bxd1 6. Bxf7+ Ke7 7. Nd5, mate.

But to play for such a trap will be a reckless gamble: After 5. ... Nxe5 Black is up a piece for a pawn. Fortunately, White can still plan the same "Legal's" mate by playing a preliminary 5. h3.

Now 5. ... Bxf3 leads to a slight edge for White, while the

natural 5. ... Bh5 allows White to zap with 6. Nxe5.

After 6. Nxe5

If Black goes for the queen, the same mate follows. Otherwise, Black is down a pawn after 6. ... Nxe5 7. Qxh5 Nxc4 8. Qb5+ Qd7 9. Qxc4.

As a ten-year-old C-player, I was devoted, as Black, to the following variation:

1. d4 d5 2. c4 e6 3. Nc3 Nf6

I was inspired then not so much by great classic games played in the Queen's Gambit Declined (Orthodox), but rather by an opportunity to meet the standard 4. Bg5 with Nbd7.

Now, 4. ... Nbd7 is a good move, but 4. ... Be7 is equally good and almost always leads to the same positions. On my level, however, 4. ... Nbd7 was a devilish trap, inviting White to grab my d-pawn after **5. cxd5** *(so far, nothing terrible)* **5.... exd5** *(the bait is dangling)* **6. Nxd5??**

6. ... Nxd5!
Zap! This pin isn't absolute, after all, and Black wins a piece for a pawn (7. Bxd8 Bb4+).

The above material is taken from my March 2003 article in *Chess Life*, which produced a record number of letters. Here is one, accompanied by a short game:

Writes Edward Trotsenko:

Recently I read, in an article titled "Opening Traps," about "Legal's Mate." I played blitz on Yahoo chess and won with Legal's Mate in quite a different way. I think it's a good idea to learn for beginners.

1. e4 e5 2. Nf3 Nc6 3. Bc4 d6 4. c3 Nf6 5. d4 exd4 6. 0-0 dxc3 7. Nxc3 Bg4
Being a pawn up, but down in development and space, Black had to prepare castling by **7. ... Be7.**
8. Bg5

8. ... Ne5? 9. Nxe5 Bxd1??
The least of all evils is **9. ... dxe5.**
True. Still after 10. Qb3, White is clearly better.
10. Bxf7+ Ke7 11. Nd5 mate.

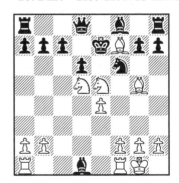

Game 9: Reader's Traps

Here is yet another letter related to my March 2003 column on opening traps.

Writes Robert Irons:

Dear GM Alburt:
Your recent column on opening traps hit home with me: The trap you enjoyed in the Queen's Gambit Declined was one of my favorites when I was a boy. Another was the Noah's Ark trap in the Ruy Lopez.

(It's called Noah's Ark because it's so old: 1. e4 e5 2. Nf3 Nc6 3. Bb5 a6 4. Ba4 Nf6 5. 0-0 Be7 6. Re1 b5 7. Bb3 d6

8. d4 exd4 9. Nxd4 Nxd4 10. Qxd4 c5

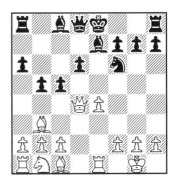

After 10. ... c5

followed by ... c4, trapping the bishop.)

Those traps used to make me feel like a master player.

These days, working two jobs and raising a family, the only opportunities I get to play are on the computer against my software programs or on the Internet. Yahoo has a site for chessplayers in its games parlor that is good for quick games. The enclosed game was played on the Yahoo site last year, and reminded me of another opening trap I used to enjoy. I have included that other trap in the analysis of the game.

I hope you enjoy it. Thank you for producing a column that "potential" masters can enjoy.

Philidor's Defense [C41]
White: Robert Irons
Black: Internet player
Yahoo site, 2002

1. e4 e5 2. Nf3 d6 3. d4 f6!?

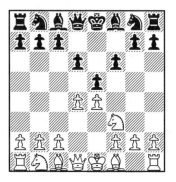

This pawn move weakens the light squares around the black king very early in the game, which is usually questionable, particularly in e-pawn opeings. It reminds me of a trap I used to enjoy when I was a kid: 1. e4 e5 2. Nf3 f6 3. Nxe5 fxe5 4. Qh5+, when Black has to choose between 4. ... g6 5. Qxe5+, dropping the h8-rook, or 4. ... Ke7 5. Qxe5+ Kf7 6. Bc4+ with a mating attack.

After
6. Bc4+

(See Game 6 — L.A.)
That approach doesn't work

here, however: 4. Nxe5 dxe5 and the knight has been given up for nothing, while if 4. dxe5 dxe5 5. Nxe5 Qxd1+ takes the wind out of White's sails. So White has to take advantage of the weakened squares from another angle.
4. Bc4
This move zeroes in on e6 and f7, while also preventing Black from playing 4. ... Be6, protecting the weak squares.
4. ... Ne7?

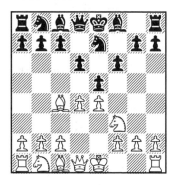

This is possibly the worst move Black can play here. Now the only escape available to the black king is on the weak light squares that White has been attacking. I saw here that if the d-file were open, Bf7+ would win the queen. This works because the king is overworked by having to protect both the weak f7-square and the queen. Given this, the next move is clearly indicated.
5. dxe5 fxe5?!
If instead 5. ... dxe5 6. Bf7+ wins. Probably best here is to re-

group with 5. ... Ng8.
6. Nxe5

6. ... dxe5

The move 6. ... d5 holds on to the queen, but leaves Black little to hope for. White has a lead in development and weak squares around the black king — an ideal attacking position.

Plus, last but not least, two extra pawns.

7. Bf7+ Kxf7 8. Qxd8, Black resigns.

White's material advantage is enough to win.

The idea of winning the queen by deflecting the defender — the king — by Bxf7+ is also present in the Smith-Morra Gambit (see Games 1 and 3).

However, in the Danish Gambit, Black can "fall" into White's trap and emerge with flying colors: 1. e4 e5 2. d4 exd4 3. c3 dxc3 4. Bc4 cxb2 (time to gather stones, or pawns) 5. Bxb2 d5! (time to give back) 6. Bxd5

6. ... Nf6! 7. Bxf7+ Kxf7 8. Qxd8

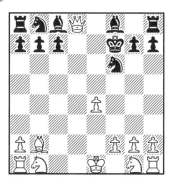

Over? Not yet! After 8. ... Bb4+ 9. Qd2! Bxd2+ 10. Nxd2

the game is even.

Game 10: To Trap or Not to Trap?

When is it okay to use traps that may be somewhat unsound? First, the potential punishment your well-prepared opponent can mete out to you should be relatively mild, while your reward (if he falls into your trap) should be much bigger. Two, at least three out of ten (30%) of your current opponents should go wrong! (When, in game after game, you are faced with the unenviable task of defending a worse position rather than enjoying the fruits of your cleverness, it's time to quit. You've outgrown this particular trap).

From my students' experience, the trap below (3. ... Nd4) works well up to the 1400 level, and even higher in blitz (even if our opponent will recall/find the right way, it may cost him too much time for his comfort).

Scott Sabol successfully used an opening trap to mate his much-higher-rated opponent — on Move 10!

Writes Mr. Sabol:

———

I don't know if this could be considered a "most instructive game," but it does show that at lower levels old tricks can work. My plan for this game was simply to have fun, no matter the outcome, and was it ever! My opponent knows this trap, knows how to avoid it, but makes a couple of pawn snatches that help him fall in, no chance. OMG.

———

Italian Game [C50]
Sylvester Kelsey (1915)
Scott Sabol (1440)
Hamilton CC G/30, 2001

1. e4 e5 2. Nf3 Nc6 3. Bc4
King pawn openings are fun, easier for me than queen pawn ones. At this point I had to decide on my plan, and came up with "Let's have fun!"
When chess is fun, we learn faster and play better.
3. ... Nd4

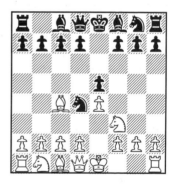

Violating opening principles by moving the same piece twice. It offers the pawn, but the smart thing for White is 0-0, and then play either c2-c3 or d2-d3. Then Black is busted. However . . .

This is the so-called Black-

burne Shilling Gambit. Supposedly Joseph Henry Blackburne would challenge club players to a game with the wager of a shilling, using this gambit.

There are a number of ways for White to respond to this move, each of which keeps the advantage – 4. Nxd4, 4. c3, 4. 0-0, 4. Nc3, or 4. d3 – because of his better development.

(Nick deFirmian in MCO *recommends 4. Nxd4 exd4 5. c3 dxc3 6. Nxc3 with clear advantage.)*

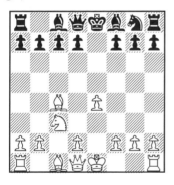

What Black wants to see is **4. Nxe5?** *as occurred in the game.*

Scott correctly replied **4. ...**

Qg5! *(By the way, I doubt that Scott's opponent "knew this trap" — if he did, why did he fall for it?)*

The game continued
5. Bxf7+

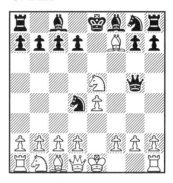

He goes for the second pawn. I just get out of the way.

5. ... Kd8

Playing for fun doesn't mean that you shouldn't play accurately — especially after your opponent already fell into your trap. Black wins material after 5. ... Ke7!, so that the f7-bishop will be hanging after the e5-knight moves, for example 6. Ng4 Kxf7.

6. Ng4

The move 6. d3 is necessary here.

Not so. 6. Ng4 is the best and only move here (6. d3 Qxe5 7. Bxg8 Rxg8). But note that this defense (Ng4) doesn't work on the fifth move: 5. Ng4 (instead of 5. Bxf7+) is met by 5. ... d5, attacking simultaneously the knight and the bishop.

6. ... Nf6

With the black king on e7 (see

my note to 5. ... Kd8) the elementary 6. ... Kxf7 would win a piece, and the game.

7. Nxf6
The simple 7. Ne3! cements White's position, and White's advantage.
7. ... Qxg2 8. Rf1 gxf6
The king pawn loses support, Again, 9. d3 is needed.
True, it's more important to guard against ... Qxe4+ than it is to protect the f3-square against the knight check.
9. Bh5 Qxe4+

10. Be2
The final blunder in a lost position.

10. ... Nf3!#
Omygoshgolly, it worked!

Crossfertilization
Quite often an idea from one opening can be successfully used in another. Edward Trotsenko, Game 8's contributor, submitted the following short game.
Wrote Edward:

My ten-year-old chess student knew this trap very well but since it happened in a very different game — in the Two Knights Defense — he fell into it.

Two Knights Defense [C50]
White: Phillip Gorokhovsky
Black: Unknown
Right Move Tmt, April 2004

1. e4 e5 2. Nf3 Nc6 3. Bc4 Nf6 4. Ng5 d5 5. exd5 Nd4

6. Nc3
The best move here is 6. c3,

with a small edge.

6. ... Nxd5

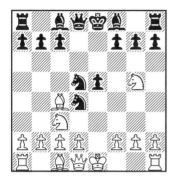

And for Black, ECO *here recommends 6. ... h6 7. Nf3 Bg4=/+.*

7. Nxd5

White is clearly better — simply up a pawn in a good position — after 7. Nxf7.

7. ... Qxg5 8. Nxc7+ Kd8

9. Nxa8

The final, decisive error. White should have tried 9. d3 and if 9. ... Qxg2? (9. ... Qg6!), then 10. Bd5.

9. ... Qxg2 10. Rf1 Qe4+

11. Be2 Nf3, Mate.

Game 11: Saved By The Trap

Traps, which abound in openings, occur and can be very effective in all stages of the game.

When surprised by an irregular opening (or any new move in an opening), first think about ways to refute it. If you are unable to do this, try steering the game into opening lines you know and play.

To refute an irregular opening means, for White, to get a clear edge; for Black, to get just the slightest advantage or even a firm equality. (For more on this subject, see Game 7)

Froilan Natividad, facing an irregular 1. Nc3, soon found himself in unfamiliar opening territory. Not surprisingly, he got a worse game and soon faced the loss of a pawn. At that moment a clever trap came to his rescue.

Pirc, Austrian Attack [B09]
White: Larry Englebretson (2207)
Black: Froilan Natividad (Unrated)
Notre Dame Invitational 2007

1. Nc3

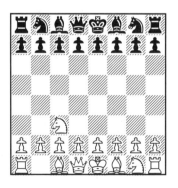

Asa Hoffman's (Asa is a New York City Master and Bobby Fischer's frequent blitz partner) favorite 1. Nc3 isn't "bad," and thus can't be truly "refuted." Still, Black equalizes with 1. ... d5, but to play this move with confidence, it isn't enough to know that it leads to equality. One should know at least one good system in the Veresov Opening (if White plays 2. d4), as well as how to meet 2. e4 — I'd recommend 2. ... dxe4, and now you need to know which (of several) moves to choose after 3. Nxe4.

Thus a second choice —transfer into a familiar opening — suggests itself. In the case of Froilan, I'd guess "his" opening is the Sicilian Dragon. Therefore, he should have played 1. ... c5, and if 2. e4, 2. ... d6 (or 2. ... Nc6 or 2. ... g6, if he prefers Accelerated Dragons). If 2. Nf3 then 2. ... g6 or 2. ... d6, and White, unless he plays e2-e4 and enters the Sicilian, can't even hope for any advantage.

1. ... g6 2. d4 Nf6 3. e4 d6

I was trying to do a Sicilian Dragon formation without c5 (this may be called a King's Indian Defense by transposition but I am not sure since the opening is irregular.)

Froilan's knowledge of openings is broad but vague and

poorly organized. Without ... c5 there is no Sicilian. The opening on the board is the Pirc; the King's Indian Defense looks a lot like the Pirc, except that White's c-pawn is on c4 —and this makes a big difference.

4. f4 Bg7

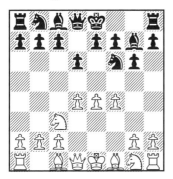

After 4. f4, I'm afraid of the same attack in the Levenfish in the Dragon where the eventual push of 5. e5 will cause Black to cramp and White has the beginning of a strong attack on Black's kingside.

If 5. e5, 5. ... dxe5 6. fxe5 Nfd7 7. Nf3 0-0 and White has a big spatial advantage.

True. Thus, Pirc players will likely play ... Nd7 without exchanging on e5: 5. ... Nfd7, preparing to undermine White's center with ... c5. The move 5. e5 is one of the main lines, and quite complex.

5. Nf3 0-0

Pirc's supreme expert GM Alex Chernin recommends the sharp 5. ... c5 (if 6. dxc5, Qa5! —

the key) and provides extensive variations in his **Pirc Alert!**.

6. Bd3 c5

I immediately counted on the queenside to relieve the tension in White's strong center.

Now it's too late, and White gets a clear edge. Better is 6. ... Nc6, or even 6. ... Na6.

7. dxc5 dxc5 8. e5

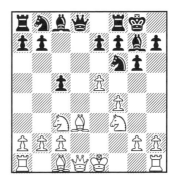

8. ... Nd5

I remember this knight move in the early opening of the Gruenfeld in the Exchange Variation. Also 8. ... Nfd7 looks very passive to me and I do not want to get cramped in this position.

Different openings can cross-fertilize each other, but it isn't the case here. In the Gruenfeld, after 1. d4 Nf6 2. c4 g6 3. Nc3 d5 4. cxd5,

After
4. cxd5

what else can Black do but re-capture the pawn?
To reject the "very passive"
(indeed!) 8. ... Nfd7, no help from
the Gruenfeld is needed.
9. Nxd5 Qxd5

10. Qe2
He's probably thinking of ad-vancing the e-pawn later with the queen support as well as prevent-ing an early queen exchange on the d-file once his white bishop moves.
10. ... Bg4
I want to develop this piece and pin his knight to have at least a counterplay.
11. Be4
Attacking the queen and the b7 pawn at the same time.
11. ... Qd7

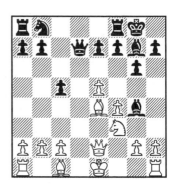

The only defense to the b7 pawn.
12. Be3
Attacking the c5 pawn and ac-tivating his rook on a1, eventu-ally placing it on d1 to attack my queen. I have no other defense for this except Rc8. If 12. ... b6??? then 13. Bxa8 and White wins.
Yes, but Black can defend the c5-pawn with 12. ... Na6.
12. ... Rc8 13. Rd1 Qc7 14. Qb5
Adding pressure on my c5 pawn.
14. ... Bxf3
I just want to simplify and do not want my bishop to be hang-ing on g4, defenseless.
15. Bxf3

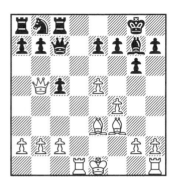

15. ... Nc6!

I made this move, knowing that if 16. Qxc5 or Bxc5, I will do 16. ... Nxe5 with an attack on the queen or bishop. Example: 16. Bxc5 Nxe5 17. Be3 Nxf3+ 18. gxf3 Qxc2 with good counterplay for Black.

If 16. Qxc5 Nxe5 17. Qxc7 Nxf3+ 18. gxf3 Rxc7 and Black has good chances since White's kingside pawn is weak.

A very clever trap, and at the same time the (objectively) best move — the ideal combination! Still, White could keep his earlier earned advantage, and win a pawn, by 16. Bxc6; e.g.: 16. ... Qxc6 17. Qxc6 Rxc6 18. Rd7.

After 18. Rd7

16. Qxc5?
Falling into the trap.

16. ... Nxe5!

17. Rd8+???
If I take the rook with my rook, then I will be queenless, so I take it with . . .

17. ... Qxd8!, White resigned.

And I now have an attack on the queen and a big material advantage — a full rook.

Well done! Black didn't panic when (probably) shocked by this rook sac (by a master!) and calmly found a winning move.

Why did Larry play 17. Rd8+, was it a bluff or a blunder? More likely the latter, as in the normal course of events (say, the 16. Qxc5 line Froilan gives to move 15) a master shouldn't lose to a 1600, even an 1800 player. In fact, he may even have some chances to win against less experienced opponent. Perhaps Larry saw a way to deflect the c8 rook, didn't check his analysis, and made a terrible blunder.

When he saw my last move, White extended his hand and resigned.

This was my first tournament and I was very happy with the result. I was told that I had just beat a USCF National Master with a Life membership and a rating of 2207 at the time. On Move 16, White should have continued adding pressure on my c5 pawn by 16. Rd5, then I can play 16. ... b6 but my knight is hanging with the support of my queen and rook. My white squares will also be weak due to the influence of White's king bishop on the long h1-a8 diagonal. *(See my comments to 15. ... Nc6 — 16. Bxc6! — LA)*

It was a one-hour tournament for each player and I spent 28 minutes while White had spent 30 minutes when he resigned. I was told later that this tournament is not rated, so I won't be getting a rating by winning this game. They just do the pairing based on the early registrants on a five-round Swiss system. I was able to win three games out of five in this tournament, not a bad start for a beginner.

Not bad at all. Froilan literally snatched victory from the jaws of looming doom. A good lesson for all players, beginners and masters alike: Don't relax in a much better position even when facing a lower-rated player. And if you are down, don't give up, watch for opportunities — you

have erred, your opponent may err too.

How To Set Up A Trap

To make a trap work, you need a good bait (in the game above, it was Black's c5-pawn). The move you want your opponent to make should look attractive for him — which means it should, at first glance, appear dangerous (to you).

Let's look at the position which happened in the game Chigorin-Schlechter, Ostende, 1905.

White is winning, but he still has to work for this. One winning plan: to play b5-b6 and then to exchange his queen and the b-pawn for the black queen. After that, the victory is automatic — White's king marches to devour Black's kingside pawns, while Black's king remains busy with White's a-pawn. Note White's goal — an exchange of queens, even at the price of a pawn.

Schlechter played **1. ... Qc7+**,

allowing **2. Qb6+**

with an apparent exchange of queens. However, after **2. ... Ka8!**, the game ended in a draw: **3. Qxc7** stalemate, or **3. Ka6 Qc8+ 4. Ka5 Qc7.**

Sometimes a trap is prepared well before the game, as it happened in Moscow, in the year 1937, the game being Reuben Fine–Michael Yudovich.
1. d4 d5 2. c4 e6 3. Nc3 Nf6 4. Nf3 c5

Yudovich prepared for the encounter by playing over a large number of Fine's games. In one of them he noticed that Fine had won by catching his opponent in an opening trap. Yudovich found, however, that Fine's trap could be refuted and so decided that in his own game with Fine he would "fall into" White's trap.
5. Bg5 cxd4 6. Nxd4 e5 7. Ndb5

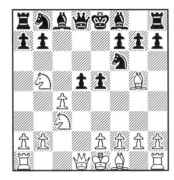

7... a6 8. Nxd5?
White has to play instead 8. Qa4, with a complicated game. Fine (at that time one of the best players in the world), however, glanced slyly at his opponent, thinking he had caught yet another inexperienced master in his trap, and played 8. Nxd5? instantaneously.

In those pre-*Informant*, not to say pre-ChessBase, days it was natural to assume that a game played in America may remain unknown in Russia, and vice versa.
8. ... axb5

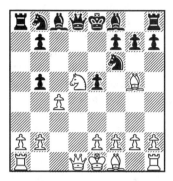

9. Nxf6+ Qxf6!

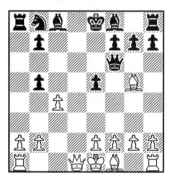

. A stunning TN! In an earlier game, Fine won after 9. ... gxf6?? 10. Qxd8+ Kxd8 11. Bxf6+

After 11. Bxf6+

But after Yudovich's move, White is lost: **10. Bxf6**

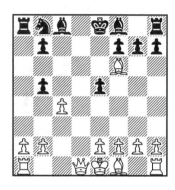

10. ... Bb4+! 11. Qd2 Bxd2+ 12. Kxd2 gxf6

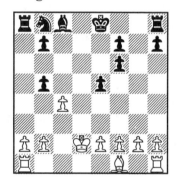

And soon Black won. (But Fine still won the tournament.)

Part III
The Art of Sacrifice

Game 12: More Often Than Not, Initiative Trumps Material

Preventing your opponent from castling is a worthy objective — but at what cost?

The game below, a draw, is all about eternal initiative vs. material struggle. Writes the generous author:

This is the game between me (Preston Herrington) and Jerry Qu, a nine year old. We both had three points gong into the final game. Jerry's rating was 1433 and mine was 1550. In all six games at this tournament, I think I had the advantage during the opening, but let it slip often. Jerry makes a mistake in the opening, but keeps his composure and looks for counterplay. If you do feature this game, maybe you could surprise Jerry and send him a book, since you sent me one in the spring of 2009. I don't have his address, but he is from San Diego, he tells me.

Queen's Pawn Opening [D02]
White: Jerry Qu (1433)
Black: Preston Herrington (1540)
National Chess Open, 2010

1. d4 Nf6 2. Nf3 d5
This is the move Fritz suggests, and it seems to equalize for Black. It prevents a quick e4 by White. If Black doesn't play an early ... d5, White can play Nc3

and e4, and 0-0-0 is attractive since White has not moved his c-pawn.
2. ... d5 is OK, and so are 2. ... g6 (King's Indian/Gruenfeld) and 2. ... e6.
3. g3

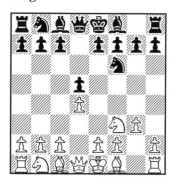

Preparing Bg2 to pressure my d-pawn.
Objectively 3. c4 is the best here, transposing into the Queen's Gambit.
3. ... c5 4. c3
Making the position the Slav with colors reversed.
Correct, and very skillful observation.
4. ... Nc6 5. Bg2 e6 6. Bf4?

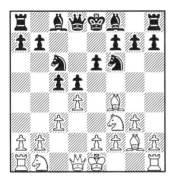
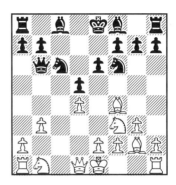

Better was 6. 0-0. Moving the c-bishop in QGD or Slav openings invites an attack on the b-pawn which has been abandoned by the bishop.

Even if White wanted to play Bf4, it would make sense to first play 6. 0-0. At least, there would be no checks on b4.

6. ... Qb6

Fritz points out that slightly better was 6. ... cxd4 first, and then 7. ... Qb6.

Correct: after 6. ... cxd4 7. cxd4 (stronger is 7. Nxd4) 7. ... Qb6 8. Qb3 loses a pawn to 8. ... Nxd4, while in the game, after 6. ... Qb6, 7. Qb3 equalizes, as noted by Preston a move later.

7. b3?

White can maintain equality with 7. Qb3.

Yes, after 7. Qb3 Qxb3 8. axb3 White's active a1-rook fully compensates for double (after 8. ... cxd4, double-isolated) b-pawns.

7. ... cxd4 8. cxd4

White will lose a pawn, and better was 8. 0-0 dxc3 9. Nxc3.

White faces a tough choice: to sacrifice a pawn with 8. 0-0 (for no compensation) or to suffer in the line 8. cxd4 Bb4+ 9. Kf1 — see Fritz's comment below.

8. ... Bb4+

Developing with a gain of time.

9. Bd2

White has lost tempi and will lose material, all the result of 6. Bf4?. Fritz prefers Nbd2, but says best is 9. Kf1, which is counterintuitive to me.

A bit confusing: how can Fritz prefer 9. Nbd2, while calling 9. Kf1 the best? After 9. Kf1, White keeps material even, but positionally Black is much better (9. ... Ne4!, restraining the b1-knight).

9. ... Nxd4

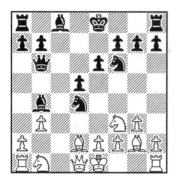

10. Nxd4?
Wasting more time, and bringing Black's queen to a dangerous center square. Better was 10. 0-0.
10. ... Qxd4!
Why the exclam, if 10. ... Qxd4 is Black's only move?
11. Bxb4

Just as good, per Fritz, was 11. 0-0. Now I have to decide whether to grab more material with 11. ... Qxa1 or to play 11. ... Qxb4+, maintaining the initiative — still a full pawn up and White without compensation or counterplay. My playing style is more

in line with ... Qxb4+, but I often miss opportunities due to undue caution. At this point Jerry offered me a draw, but I thought I had everything going for me, and I was playing a lower rated player, so I declined.
11. ... Qxa1
I decided to be greedy and grab the material. I am pleased that Fritz thinks this is the best move. However, in retrospect I regretted this move. I reassured myself that my queen could not be trapped after 12. Bc3 Qxa2. I failed to take into account the counterplay White would have by maintaining a bishop on the a3-f8 diagonal, preventing Black from castling.
The Question is: would Black be able to neutralize White's initiative and, in particular, castle by hand? If yes, grabbing the exchange (in addition to a pawn) was a right decision — as Fritz thinks (and so do I).
12. Qc2 Qd4 13. Ba3 Bd7

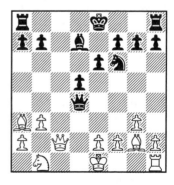

14. e3
Dislodging my queen from

her powerful perch on d4.

14. ... Qb6

Maintaining control over c5. If instead 14. ... Qe5? 15. Qc5! threatens mate and forces 15. ... Kd8.

15. 0-0

15. ... Rc8

Developing the rook with a gain of time. Fritz suggests starting a kingside attack with 15. ... h5 followed by ... h4.

Fritz's suggestion is really about activating the king's rook (the attack per se *isn't there, as White's king is very safe). Another interesting plan was to castle long (after 15. ... Bc6).*

16. Qd2 Ne4

Bringing the knight to a nice central square, again with a gain of time.

17. Bxe4

The best move. I was expecting his queen to continue to run — for example 17. Qb2 or 17. Qe1, either of which is answered by 17. ... f6.

17. Bxe4! is indeed the best move — and the only move which keeps the struggle going.

17. ... dxe4 18. Rd1

White is mobilizing his pieces, with the exception of the knight, who is keeping the bishop well-defended. Black is up the exchange and a pawn, but his king is not yet safe.

18. ... Rd8

Defending the bishop a second time. Alternatively, 18. ... Bc6 was fine, too.

19. Bd6!?

Fritz suggests attacking with either 19. Qc3, 19. Qc2, or 19. Nc3. Also good was 19. Rc1. *All these moves are OK — but Black is nevertheless somewhat better.*

19. ... e5?

My thinking was that 19. ... e5 opened up my bishop to go to g4 or h3, and I expected 20. Bxe5. Fritz says Black is fine after 19. ... Bb5 or 19. ... Bc6 or 19. ... f6. *Black's goal is to connect rooks, after which his material advantage should prevail. All moves Fritz gives serve this purpose; 19. ... f6 is perhaps the most straightforward.*

20. Qc3!

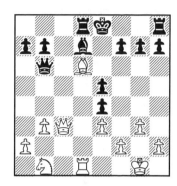

Now Fritz has the game even, but I am not enjoying it. I have a material advantage but a king that's under attack.

20. ... Be6?

I had to play 20. ... f6 to hold equality. I honestly don't remember a good reason for playing 20. ... Be6. I probably thought I was attacking the bishop twice, and the bishop was pinned.

Yes, 20. ... f6 is a must. After 21. Bc7(what else?) White regains material, but the following R+B vs R+N ending slightly favors Black.

The course of this game conforms to the old wisdom: it's easier to attack than to defend — which is especially true below Master level. Still, players of all levels could, and should, improve both attacking and defensive skills, and here this game, starting with Move 7, can be quite helpful.

21. Qxe5!

And now my position is in trouble. I was very much wishing

I had played 11. ... Qxb4+ and maintained the initiative. My g-pawn is now under attack, his bishop is well defended, my king is squirming, and he hasn't even activated his knight.

21. ... Rg8

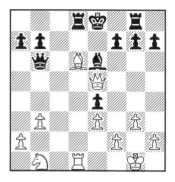

I knew I would have to give back the exchange with ... Rxd6

very soon, but I preferred to guard my g-pawn first. I have no hope of castling. Of course, I am dreaming of exchanging queens and simplifying to an endgame.

22. Rd4

Freeing his bishop to move without my playing ... Rxd1. A better way to accomplish this was 22. Nc3, which also develops his last piece.

(Correct! — L.A.)

As I began to ponder my deteriorating position, Jerry offered a draw again, and this time I eagerly accepted. The happy ending to the story is that we both ended the tournament in the plus with 3.5 points, and we both gained rating points from the tourney.

The course of this game conforms to the old wisdom: it's easier to attack than to defend — which is especially true below Master level. Still, players of all levels could, and should, improve both attacking and defensive skills,

Game 13: An "Iffy" Sacrifice

This game is an excellent illustration of how the initiative works — and thus how important it is for the opposite side to play very precisely. Even a dubious sacrifice which opens an opponent's king can be very effective over the board,

The games played by great "romantics" such as Morphy and Tal demonstrate the value of initiative, and the value of attack vs. material count. At the class level, a speculative sacrifice can often be effective over the board, later refutations by Fritz notwithstanding.

Writes the winner of this game, Bruce Radford:

I'm 56 years old. Chess books don't talk much about us aging players, but we're out there, battling against declining stamina and those ever-encroaching senior moments. Here's a game where I "blacked out" in the opening, forgetting the correct line (which I knew cold) and wrecking my position. In desperation I tried an iffy sacrifice, and got lucky.

French Defense [C21]
White: Joel Fagliano (1435)
Black: Bruce Radford (1500)
Liberty Bell Open 2006

1. e4 e6 2. d4 d5 3. e5 c5 4. c3 Nc6 5. Nf3 Qb6 6. a3

6. ... Bd7
Also good is 6. ... Nh6 (see below) as well as 6. ... c4. All these moves are supposed to lead to equality, while after 6. ... a5 White, according to ECO, gets a small edge.
7. b4 cxd4 8. cxd4 Rc8 9. Bb2

So far so good. Of course, in *Play the French*, John Watson prefers 6. ... Nh6 (as Joel told me

after the game). Watson advises against Black's line here, saying it relies too much on tricks, and maybe he's right. Black intends 9. ... Na5 and then Nc4, taking advantage of the temporary pin on White's b-pawn to bootstrap the QN to c4.

For example, in a later game as Black in this tournament I played 9. ... Na5, 10. Nc3? (Nbd2) Nc4 11. Bxc4 Rxc4, and enjoyed good play against White's light-square weakness.

But here, in our game, all of a sudden I suffered a "senior moment." I just blacked out and somehow imagined that if 9. ... Na5 is okay, then think of how much better it would be if preceded by a solid developing move — wrong!

9. ... Nge7? 10. Nbd2

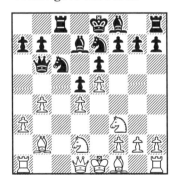

10. ... Na5

If Bruce saw what's coming (11. Rc1) he may have found an interesting sacrifice: 10. ... Nf5 11. Nb3 Bxb4+ 12. axb4 Qxb4+.

After 12. ... Qxb4+

11. Rc1

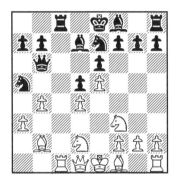

Whoa, what was I thinking? By giving White extra time to develop his queenside, now 11. ... Nc4 just loses a pawn. Even so, perhaps I should have plowed ahead and taken my lumps. Instead, I now tried to retreat and undo the damage, which as we all know never works in chess. So my next two moves are terrible.

11. ... Rxc1 12. Qxc1 Nac6 13. Nb3

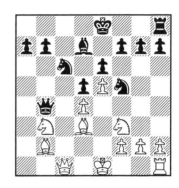

At this point my position is nearly resignable. White will jam his knight down my throat at c5, forcing me to take it off soon with my dark-squared bishop, which, as any French player knows, is better left on the board. *Black is worse (+/-), but far from being lost.*
13. ... Nf5 14. Bd3
Suddenly a light bulb flicked on. White's move somehow looked like a mistake, but why? Then I realized: the bishop was loose! My misguided moves had deflected White's queen to c1, leaving Bd3 hanging, not to mention also the knight on b3. Maybe I could turn that into something. I knew I had to try something drastic, and right away.
Objectively, 14. ... Bxb4+ loses, while 14. ... Be7, followed by castling, leads to the above-mentioned "+/-". But dubious, even faulty, sacrifices often work in practice.
14. ... Bxb4+ 15. axb4 Qxb4+

Truly a crucial moment! If only White had realized this and used the time to find the relatively simple 16. Qc3, the game would be almost over, as White's extra piece is much more valuable than Black's a7 and b7 pawns.
16. Nbd2 Nfxd4 17. Nxd4 Nxd4

Now 18. Ba3 would put a real damper on Black's fun, sending the queen running and trapping Black's king in the center and his rook in the corner. Black could answer 18. ... Nb3, but 19. Qc8+ Bxc8 20. Bxb4 looks absolutely winning for White. I had over-

looked all of this. My attempt at counterplay had a few holes in it.

Luckily for me however, both sides were banging out the captures moves in rapid fire. That created a sort of momentum, leading each side to slam down the pieces even faster, and continue trading on d4 until the last man was standing. Lucky me, 18. Ba3 was never played.

Even stronger than 18. Ba3 is the simple 18. 0-0, keeping Ba3 in reserve. ("The threat is stronger than the execution" — Nimzovich)

18. Bxd4 Qxd4

Here is where I had hoped to be when I was sacking the piece. I have three pawns in trade, plus my queen is forward and centralized, with White's king still in the center. The hanging bishop on d3 makes it all possible.

The "hanging bishop on d3" became a factor only after White's errors on the 16th and 18th moves.

19. Qc7 0-0

I am content here just to castle and trade my bad bishop for White's good one. I had overlooked the desperado move 20. Bxh7+, but it's no good here, since White must lose either a knight or a rook after 20. ... Kxh7 21. Qxd7 Qxe5+.

Stronger was 19. ... Qxd3, forcing White to go for an immediate draw after 20. Qb8+ Ke7

After 20. ... Ke7

21. Qd6+! (21. Qxh8? Bb5) 21. ... Kd8 22. Qb8+ Bc8 23. Qd6+ Ke8 24. Qc7.

20. Qxd7 Qxd3 21. Qxb7 Qc3

I lose a pawn, but the game now is all about White's exposed king and undeveloped rook.

22. Kd1

Ugly, but probably forced

sooner or later. So what should Black do now? Try for a quick knockout by cashing in the passed a-pawn, or consolidate and keep White off-balance?

22. ... Qxe5 23. Qxa7

I feared that pushing the passed a-pawn right away might actually prove too slow. It might just draw White's men out in the open where the extra piece would tell. Meanwhile, the e5-pawn had me worried, as it might come in handy for White to support a kingside attack. So I create a fortress while still keeping my options open and White's pieces bottled up. All the same I winced when White gobbled up my a-pawn. Was I doing the right thing?

Objectively — at least as it seems to me — White is slightly better in both cases, thus my preference for 19. ... Qxd3. The choice between 22. ... Qxe5 and 22. ... a5 is a very close one. 22. ... Qxe5 is safer, 22 ... a5 more ambitious.

23. ... h6

24. Nf3

This knight move leaves the White king without cover and just nudges the Black queen to a better square. Was it better to play 24. h4, to prepare Re1, or to lift the rook to h3? All I know is that White must develop his rook or die.

White's last move was an error, while the move recommended by Bruce, 24. h4 (to prepare Re1), is stronger. Still, Black isn't in any real danger — even a knight+3 pawns vs. 5 pawns ending looks rather drawish here.

24. ... Qb2

Black eyes Rc8-c1. White is in peril.

25. Qe3

Guarding c1, but surrendering the a-file.

The losing move. 25. Nd2 (or 25. Re1 Rc8 26. Nd2) 25. ... Rc8 26. Re1 Rc1+ 27. Ke2 Qe5+, losing a pawn on h2, was a likely draw, albeit here it was White who would be on the defensive.

25. ... Ra8, and Black won.

A lucky escape for Black.

Game 14: *THE* Sacrifice

The sacrifice Bxh7+ (for Black, Bxh2+) is a common one, and thus exceedingly important — master it!

The game below initially attracted my special attention for two reasons: first, the author submitted his lost game; second, his opponent was Al Lawrence, co-author of my *Comprehensive Chess Course: From Beginner to Master* series.

My attention was well rewarded! Writes Tom Beechey:

Although I lost the game I was hoping you could shed some light on it. I used a Fidelity Mach 3 table top computer to help with the analysis.

Sicilian Wing Gambit [B20]
Al Lawrence (2000)
Tom Beechey (1548)
3rd Sat. Open, Newtown, CT.

1. e4 c5 2. b4

In my 20+ years of playing

competitive chess I don't remember having to play against this move. *MCO #13* gives one line from GMs Bronstein & Benko, 1949, Moscow versus Budapest 1949, where Black captures the pawn: 2. ... cxb4 3. a3 d5 4. exd5 Qxd5

After 4. ... Qxd5

5. Nf3 e5 6. axb4 Bxb4 7. Na3 Bxa3 8. Bxa3 Nc6 9. c4 Qd8 10. Qb1 Nge7 giving Black equal chances.

Having never played against this opening and not being able to check my trusty *MCO* during the game I did not feel comfortable giving up on the d4 square.

If you play the Sicilian, you need to know a few simple lines against the Wing Gambit (like the one above) starting with 2. ... cxb4!. In a reversal of usual roles, it is White who must seek the equality. Note that 5. axb4

After 5. axb4

(instead of 5. Nf3) loses to 5. ... Qe5+ (double-attack), while after the overly persistent 5. Nf3 Bg4 (instead of 5. ... e5) axb4! Bxf3 7. Qxf3 Qe5+ (relatively better is 7. ... Qxf3, albeit the ending favors the better developed side, White) 8. Kd1 Qxa1? 9. Qxb7, White reaps a richer harvest.

However — facing a novelty — Tom made a reasoned and good choice, 2. ... b6, second only to the best, 2. ... cxb4.

2. ... b6 3. Nf3

To prove that the possible disappearance of b-pawns favors him, White has to play very accurately! Better was 3. bxc5 bxc5 4. Nc3, prophylactically protecting

the e4-pawn and thus ready to meet 4. ... Bb7 with 5. Rb1.

3. ... Bb7 4. bxc5 bxc5
Another possible continuation would to be to capture the e-pawn with the bishop: 4. ... Bxe4 5. cxb6 Qxb6 6. Nc3 Nf6 etc.
4. bxc5 bxc5 5. Nc3 Nc6 6. Rb1 Rb8

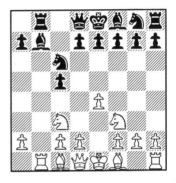

Now this defense — contesting, potentially, the b-file — becomes possible (see my note to 3. Nf3.)

7. Bc4
After the to-be-expected 7. ... e6, this bishop looks into a stone wall (e6-pawn protected by f7-pawn); in fact, it will soon relocate to b5. Thus, 7. Bb5!

7. ... e6 8. 0-0 Be7 9. d3 d6 10. Bf4 Nf6 11. e5

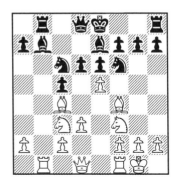

even) forcing the black king to f8 and thus gaining a tempo, and a small edge. (If 13. ... Nd7 14. Bxe5 Rc8, then 15. Qg4! — but not 15. Bxg7? Rg8, and now Black successfully exploits the g-file).
13. ... dxe5 13. Bb5+ Kf8 14. Nxe5

11. ... Nxe5
More natural, and stronger is 11. ... dxe5, expanding Black's options — and limiting White's. For instance, after 12. Nxe5 Nxe5

After
12. ...
Nxe5

13. Bb5+, Black can avoid 13. ... Kf8 in favor of 13. ... Ned7. If 14. Bxb8 Qxb8 15. Bc6, then 15. ... Bxc6, and Black's three minors are stronger than the white queen. Thus, White should play 13. Bxe5 Bd6 and only now 14. Bb5+, allowing the black king to move not to f8 (see my next comment) but to e7.
12. Bxe5
Creative — and wrong. White should play the natural 12. Nxe5 dxe5 13. Bb5+! (after 13. Bxe5 Bd6 14. Bb5+ Ke7! the game is

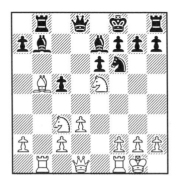

14. ... Qd4
Be careful what you wish for — you may get it! White clearly aimed to get this position, denying Black castling and driving Black's king to f8. But it is White who must be very careful now! The only defense here is 15. Nc6! Bxc6 16. Bxc6, indirectly defending the c3-knight. The natural-looking defense 15. Qe1 (as in the game) loses material.
15. Qe1 Bd6

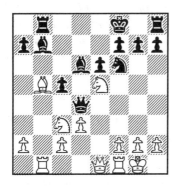

16. Nc6

As 16. Nc6 (the game) loses at least two pawns, for no compensation, in the quite obvious way, White's best practical chance to somewhat muddy the waters was 16. Nd7+ Nxd7 17. Bxd7.

16. ... Bxc6 17. Bxc6 Rxb1 18. Nxb1

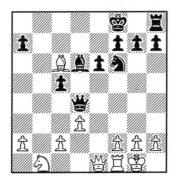

The crucial moment!
18. ... Ke7
Black missed a simple, and topical, 18. ... Bxh2+ 19. Kxh2 Qh4+! 20. Kg1 Ng4,

After
20. ... Ng4

and to avoid mate in one, White has to give away his queen (21. Qe5) with a completely lost position. Relatively better (for White) is 19. Kh1 Qh4 20. g3 Bxg3+ with (at least) two extra pawns, and excellent winning chances (for Black).

19. Qa5 Nd5
(? — L.A.)
Another possible continuation is: 19. ... Rc8 20. Qxa7+ Rc7 21. Qa4 Bxh2+ 22. Kh1 Bd6 23. g3.

The line above leads to equality, so why give up a pawn with Nd5?

20. Bxd5 Qxd5 21. Qxa7+ Kf6 22. Qa4 Qh5

23. f4
I'd prefer here the modest (and safe) 23. g3, but 23. f4 is

also fine (and provokes Black's hyperactive reaction).

23. ... g5

This is a pure case of tunnel vision on my part. I'm so happy with the potential attack on the h2 square that I overlook the pin on the black king which will cost Black an important tempo. Probably better is to play the rook to b8 and deal with White's queen infiltrating via c6. I put this position into the computer and let it play out: 23. ... Qd5 24. Nc3 Qd4 and the queens are removed. Ultimately Black recaptures the pawn on the a file but loses the game.

24. Nd2 Bxf4 25. g3 Qg4 26. Ne4+

26. ... Kg7 27. Nf2

Winning a piece. An excellent maneuver!

27. ... Qf3 28. gxf4 gxf4 29. Qe4 Qe3 30. Qxe3 fxe3

At this point the game is essentially over but we were playing sudden death and the queens were still on the board.

31. Ne4 Rb8 32. Re1 Rb2

33. Re2

Of course. In the ending, when ahead in material, don't trade too many pawns. Now the end is very near.

33. ... Rxa2 34. Kg2, White resigned.

My advice: Remember the bishop sacrifice on h7 (h2)! It will win, and save, many, many games for you.

Part IV
Attack & Defense

Games 15 & 16: Attacking Your Computer, Morphy-style

Chess is beautiful and exciting

I would like to submit two games for consideration in your column, *Back to Basics*. They were both played against computer programs, but I believe they are both very instructive.

—Michael Bligh

Yes, I've found these games, and Mike's annotations, very instructive indeed. I especially like his conclusions at the end.

Usually, I prefer to work with one well-annotated game, but these are relatively short and thematically connected, so I'm making an exception (most of the rules of chess allow exceptions, don't they?)

Ruy Lopez [C90]
White: Mike Bligh (1554)
Black: GNU Chess

1. e4 e5 2. Nf3 Nc6 3. Bb5 a6 4. Ba4 Nf6 5. 0-0 Be7 6. Re1 b5 7. Bb3 d6 8. c3 0-0 9. d3
This move is a bit quiet, better is d4.
Most common move here is 9. h3.
9. ... Bg4

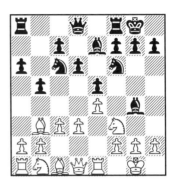

10. Be3
Better is 10. Nbd2, starting the knight's tour without delay.
10. ... Na5 11. Bc2 h6
An unnecessary weakening of the kingside. Black would be happy to trade his e7 bishop for the e3 bishop.
12. Nbd2 c5 13. h3 Bh5

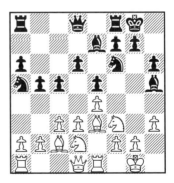

14. Rc1
A waste of time — or worse, as White's queen rook is well placed on a1 (a2-a4 is one of the

most common of White's tools in the Ruy).

14. ... Nc6 15. Nf1 Bg6

16. Qd2

I'd prefer the standard 16. Ng3, aiming to reach the f5 square.

16. ... Qa5

This move appears to create some problems for White, but it misplaces the black queen, as will be demonstrated in a few moves.

17. Bb3 c4 18. dxc4

18. ... Bxe4

Safer is 18. ... Nxe4.

19. Bxh6

This sacrifice is risky, but it is based on the lack of coordination by Black's kingside pieces.

This position should be better left to Fritz (on its highest level) to analyze! Black may play 19. ... gxh6 and hope that he is OK after 20. Qxh6 bxc4; in turn: White can employ an in-between move with 20. cxb5, keeping the a2-g8 diagonal open for his bishop..

19. ... Bxf3 20. gxf3 gxh6 21. Qxh6

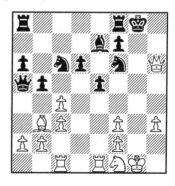

21. ... bxc4

It's time to assess what White has accomplished by sacrificing two pawns.

(Strictly speaking, a piece for two pawns. — L.A.)

To begin, the black king is trapped in the corner of the board, his pieces are not coordinated for defense, and his queen is far removed from the action. White has a strong attack to finish the game, due to the open knight file, the weakness of the white squares around the black king, and the previously-mentioned problems with Black's piece placement.

Black's best defense is 21. ... Nh7.

22. Ne3

The point. Black does not have enough tempos to bring up defenders.

22. ... cxb3

Suicide, but Black is still lost after 22. ... e4 23. Kh1 Nh7 24. Rg1+ Bg5 25. Rxg5 Qxg5 26. Rg1.

23. Nf5

The rest is simple.

23. ... Nh5 24. Kh1 Qd8 25. Rg1+ Bg5 26. Rxg5+ Qxg5 27. Qxg5+ Kh8 28. Qxh5+ Kg8 29. Rg1 mate.

Sicilian Defense [B44]
White: Mike Bligh (1554)
Black: Fritz 6 (1800)

1. e4 c5 2. Nf3 Nc6 3. d4 cxd4 4. Nxd4 e6 5. Be2

Look into ECO for more common (and better) moves.

5. ... Nf6

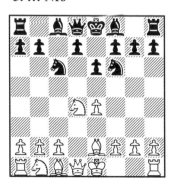

6. Bg5

This loses a pawn — for only

partial compensation — after 6. ... Qa5+. Instead, Black makes a series of bad moves which only serve to centralize White's queen.)
6. ... d5 7. exd5 Nxd4 8. Qxd4 Qxd5 9. Bxf6 gxf6

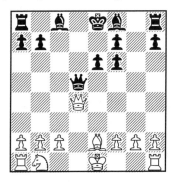

10. Qxf6

If Mr. Bligh thought during the game that the line he gives below favors Black,(see his note after 10. ... Rg8) he should have gone into a better ending by playing 10. Qxd5.
10. ... Rg8
Black is running from paper tigers. Better is 10. ... Qxg2 11. Bf3 Qg7 12. Qxg7 Bxg7, when Black retains the initiative and the slight advantage of the two bishops. Now White will conclude his development with tempo, building up a strong attack.
If this (11. Bf3) were White's only choice, then 10. Qxf6 (instead of 10. Qxd5) was an obvious mistake. However, White can,

after 10. ... Qxg2, try 11. Rf1, preserving an option to play, at the right moment, Bb5+.
11. Nc3

11. ... Bb4??
Black could have saved himself with 11. ... Qd8 12. Qf3 Bg7 with a slight advantage to White.
More than slight: after 11. ... Qd8 White is up a pawn.
Instead, the computer gives White another tempo to bring up more forces, and this costs the game.
12. Rd1 Bxc3+ 13. bxc3 Qa5

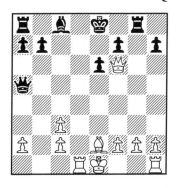

14. Bb5+
The shot. Now Black's

fortress crumbles in rapid fashion
Well done.
14. ... Bd7 15. Bxd7+
An even faster win is 15.
Rxd7.
**15. ... Kf8 16. Bxe6 Qh5 17.
Rd7 Qe5+ 18. Qxe5 Rc8 19.
Rxf7+ Ke8 20. Bd5+ Kd8 21.
Qe7 mate.**

The things that I learned from
these games were:
1. It is important to play dynamic, aggressive chess. Once you become passive, you are at the mercy of your opponent.
True — in most cases.
2. How much material is on the board is not nearly as important as how much the material on the board is accomplishing.
True.
3. Chess is beautiful and exciting, so have FUN with it!
Absolutely true!

Game 17:
Ignore Threats at Your Peril

A good question to ask:
"What are the implications of my opponent's last move?"

Writes Robert Getty:

1276 versus 1900. This game shows the dangers of getting locked into a plan without constantly re-evaluating the position: twice I have a win that is overlooked.

King's Indian Defense
Saemisch Variation [E81]
White: Zach Kinney (1900)
Black: Robert Getty (1276)
2007 Armed Forces Open

1. d4 Nf6
I've never learned the Queen's Gambit, so I always respond to 1. d4 with a King's Indian.
2. c4 d6 3. Nc3 g6 4. e4

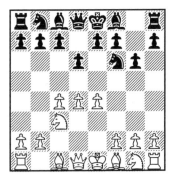

4. ... c5
I'm no longer playing from an opening book; I'm just instinc-tively reacting to not liking White's pawn center.

Not liking White's center shows Robert's good positional sense; what he needs is a bit more knowledge of the openings he plays. Here is the King's Indian in a nutshell: Black gives his opponent full freedom to build a strong (or even super-strong, with pawns on c4, d4, e4, and f4 or f3) pawn center — and, more broadly, to develop his pawns and pieces any way he wants, for at least the first six moves.

Black meanwhile plays ... Nf6, ... g6, ... Bg7, ... d6, and ... 0-0, achieving two out of the three usual opening goals: harmonious development of pieces (a fianchettoed bishop is usually very good in KI) and castling. After that Black will challenge White's center with either ... e5 or ... c5, depending on how White used his first six moves. 4. ... c5 is a small error, as the ending after 5. dxc5 dxc5 (a common trick, 5. ... Qa5, doesn't work here: 6. cxd6 Nxe4 7. Qd4 — the g7-bishop is badly missing) 6. Qxd8+ Kxd8 7. e5 favors White.

5. d5
Now it's back to theory. Note that if Black wants to get this position, he can and should do it via a different move order, for in-

stance 1. d4 Nf6 2. c4 c5 3. d5 g6 4. Nc3 d6 5. e4. Exactly the position reached in the game!

5. ... Bg7 6. Bd3 0-0 7. Nge2

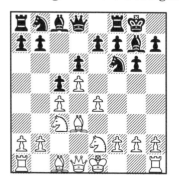

7. ... a6

Better was to play 7. ... e6 and then ... exd5, or even 7. ... Nbd7, as Black played on his next move.

8. f3 Nbd7 9. Be3

I would prefer to preserve the light-squared bishop, e.g. by playing 9. Ng3!?.

9. ... Ne5 10. Qd2 Rb8 11. a4 Bd7

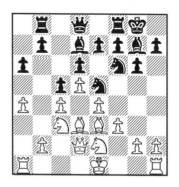

12. Kf2

With Black ready to open the center, placing the king on f2 means asking for trouble. Why

not castle?

12. ... e6 13. b3 exd5 14. exd5 Re8

15. h3

Defending against 15. ... N(any)g4+ 16. fxg4 Nxg4+, with an extra pawn and great position for Black.

15. ... Nxd3+

The sharp 15. ... Nh5 deserves attention — but Robert's choice is logical, solid — and good.

16. Qxd3 Re7 17. Rac1

17. ... Qc7

The queen on c7 will be out of action. Interesting here was 17. ... Qf8 with an option later to play ... Bh6.

**18. Bg5 Rbe8 19. Rhe1 h6
20. Bh4 Bf5 21. Qd2 g5 22. Bg3**

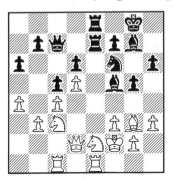

22. ... Nh5?!
What real value is there in chasing the bishop?
Perhaps Black should relocate his knight to e5.
23. Bh2

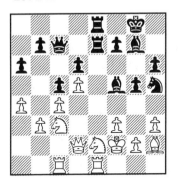

I attacked the bishop, so I expect it to move.
23. ...Qd7? 24. g4!
How can I miss this? Everyone knows that when determining your move, one of the questions you have to ask yourself is, "What are the implications of my opponent's last

move?"
24. ... Nf6 25. gxf5 Qxf5 26. Bxd6
I'm down material to a higher rated player. Right now, I need to attack while I still have a chance.
26. ... Re3

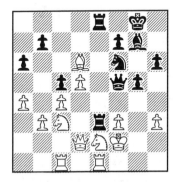

27. Bxc5?
My moment of truth. White could have moved his knight to g1 to swap off rooks, or even swapped his queen and h-pawn for my rooks. Instead, he has let me back into the game. Here, I'm thinking that I can snatch a draw from the jaws of defeat, and develop a situation for a perpetual check with the white king looking exposed. When given the opportunity for a win, I turn it down in a misguided attempt for a draw.
27 ... Qxf3+??
27. ... Rxf3+! 28. Kg1 Qxh3 29. Nf4 Rxe1+ 30. Rxe1 Rxf4 31. Qxf4 (31. Re2 Rf1#) 31. ... gxf4.
28. Kg1

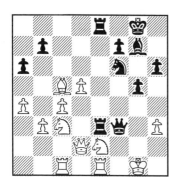

28. ... Rd3 29. Qc2 Ree3
I'm still looking for a perpetual check, and willing to give up the exchange to remove defenders.

Even here it's not too late to remove a defender for free — to capture the h3-pawn.
30. Rf1 Qxh3 31. Bxe3

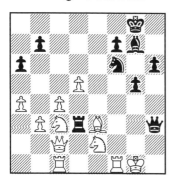

This move loses, demonstrating how strong Black's attack became after the suicidal 27. Bxc5 — all Black's real and imagined inaccuracies notwithstanding.
31. ... Rxe3
Why not take on e3 with check, with a perpetual check

both guaranteed and easy — and a win (for Black) very likely?
32. Qf5 Ng4 33. Qxf7+

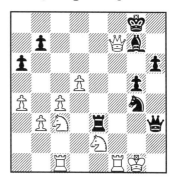

Things are starting to look really bad.
33. ... Kh7
Black can avoid further checks with 33. ... Kh8.
34. Qf5+ Kh8 35 Qc8+ Kh7 36. Qc7?

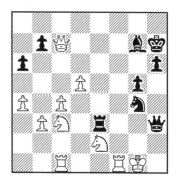

I can STILL climb back into this game. Right now, all I'm thinking is that my king looks safer on h5 on the other side of the pawns. However, I'm still threatening mate with Qh2 if I can just get his queen off of the

h2-b8 diagonal. The move 36. ... Re7! provides the potential to get the bishop to e5 where it is covered by the knight: 36. ... Re7 37. Qd6 *(37. Qg3 Bd4+ — L.A.)* Rd7 38. Qb8 Be5 39. Qxe5 Nxe5.
36. ... Kg6? 37. c5 Rd3 38. Ne4

38. ... Kh5??

Immediately loses.

Robert missed another good check with his queen, on the same e3-square.

39. N2g3+ Kh4 40. Nf5+, Black resigned

With Qf7# staring at him. After this game, my opponent said to me, "You pressed me really hard; how can you be a 1276?" I looked at him and asked, "Did I find the win?" After his "no," I said, "THAT is why I'm a 1276."

Self-criticism is OK — especially if combined with a program for improvement. Study openings (a little); watch opponent's threats — and remember, checks (being very forceful) are often the best moves!

Game 18: Inspired by Fischer

Thirteen-year-old Nolan Hendrickson entitled his letter "Blitz is for Risk Takers ... Only!" As you'll soon see, despite the risks, the quality of play is quite impressive.

King's Indian Attack [A08]
White: Nolan Hendrickson
                    (unrated)
Black: Crafty, the Computer

1. e4 e6 2. d3 d5 3. Nd2

My style is close to that of Fischer. I try to avoid playing the French Defense as White and go for the King's Indian formation.

3 ... Nf6

If you, as Black, wish to avoid "Fischer's Wrath," you can place this knight on e7 — after developing your dark-square bishop on either d6 or g7 (e.g., 3 ... c5 4. Ngf3 Nc6 5. g3 Bd6 6. Bg2 Nge7, or 5. ... g6 6. Bg2 Bg7 7. 0-0 Nge7).

4. Ngf3 c5 5. g3 Nc6 6. Bg2

Even now it isn't too late to preempt White's attack by fianchettoing the f8-bishop. Then White's e4-e5 will likely lead to a loss of that pawn. Theory's verdict? — unclear (which is okay for Black).

6 ... Be7 7. 0-0 0-0

White wants to play e5 and further expand space, and Black has little to do that will stop this.

8. Re1

The move e4-e5 almost always transposes.

8. ... b5

A good choice. Black plans to start building up counterplay now, before White's attack gets too strong.

9. e5 Nd7 10. h4

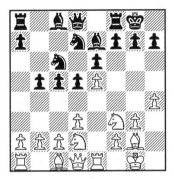

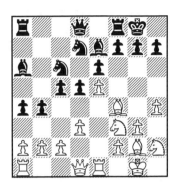

From here I hope to go to Nf1 via h2 and later hop into the g4 square.

I'd prefer to play 10. Nf1 first, and then 11. h4. Usually —as in this game — it's a simple transposition (into the same position) but if Black plays 10 ... Qc7, or even 10. ... f6, Nf1 seems more useful for White than h4.

10. ... a5 11. Nf1 b4 12. N1h2 Ba6

Opening theory is fizzled out by now, and both sides have a clear plan of playing on opposite sides of the board.

13. Bf4

This move develops the bishop as well as protecting the e-pawn from further harassment from the possible 13. ... Qc7.

13. ... a4

14. Ng5

Here I want Black to provoke h7-h6, a weakness in its kingside even if I have to move the knight back where it came from.

Other plans are: 14. h5 and then h5-h6; 14. a3 (trying to check Black's queenside advance).

14. ... h6

Perhaps premature, but this will need to be done after I play Qh5 anyway.

15. Ngf3

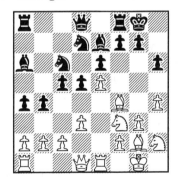

More common is 15. Nh3, planning Qh5.

15 ... Bb5

This move might be okay, but it is definitely a timewaster, maybe the computer should have further defended his king by moving his rook to e8 and resting a knight on f8 *(Not a knight, but rather bishop — to protect the h6-pawn and to enable, if needed, the freeing ... f6 — LA)* or maybe bring the queen to b6.
A time waster in a sharp position can't be okay.

16. Qd2
I'm preparing potential pressure *(sacrifice — L.A.)* on h6.

16. ... Qc7
Better was 16. ... Re8, challenging White to sacrifice on h6 in not-so-clear circumstances.

17. Ng4

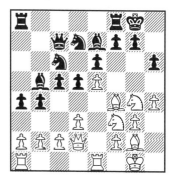

17 ... c4
This counterplay is too little, too late. I'd prefer 17 ... h5, testing the opponent to see whether he would dare to play 18. Nf6+, with a big edge, rather than the meek 18. Ngh2.

18. Bxh6 gxh6 19. Qxh6!

Knight takes h6 would make Black's king happier.
Indeed. After a long-thought-about and well-prepared piece sacrifice, White is winning.

19 ... Qd8
Black has to take extreme measures because of the knight coming to f6.
The threat was first Ng5, as in the game. For instance: 19 ... cxd3 20. Ng5! Bxg5 21. hxg5 and NOW 22. Nf6+ is indeed a winning threat. Black's best practical chance here: 19. ... f6, albeit White's attack still should prevail.

20. Ng5! Bxg5 21. hxg5

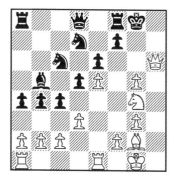

21 ... Ne7?
I thought 21. ... f6 would
have been solid.
*No. After 22. exf6 Rf7 (to stop
a mate in one) 23. Qg6+ Kf8 24.
Nh6 White wins; 24. g6 also
wins.*
**22. Nf6+ Nxf6 23. gxf6 Nf5
24. Qg5+**
If my attack fails, I at least
have a draw.
24. ... Kh7

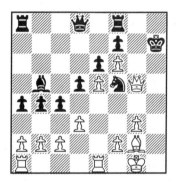

25. Be4!!
Successfully ends the game.
*True. By the way, 24 ... Kh8
also loses, for instance by 25. g4
(or 25. Bh3) — as 25. ... Rg8
leads to a mate in two after 26.
Qh5+.*
25. ... Qxf6
Black's options are slim. If he
takes my bishop, then dxe4 and
the knight is pinned because of
mate on g7. If he gives up the
knight, mate will soon follow.
*This is the one and only error
Nolan makes in his annotations.
After 25 ... dxe4*

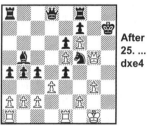

After
25. ...
dxe4

*26. dxe4 is very bad, as 26. ...
Rg8 ends White's attack (if 27.
Qh5+, then 27. ... Nh6). However, White wins easily by simply
playing (after 25. ... dxe4) 26.
Kg2, with the winning Rh1+ to
follow. Also winning, but by a
longer route, is the fancier 26.
Rxe4 (with the threat of 27. Rh4+
Nxh4 28. Qg7 checkmate) 26. ...
Rg8 27. Rh4+ Nxh4 28. Qh5
checkmate. (Black's . ... Rg8 cuts
off the only available retreat for
the king.) I guess Nolan would
have found 26. Kg2, if Crafty had
played 25. ... dxe4.*
26. exf6 dxe4

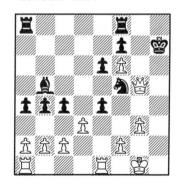

27. dxe4
*This is Nolan's only bad move
in this game.*
I believe rook captures pawn

is a quicker win, because of yet another possible sacrifice on h4 with the rook! *Correct. Even simpler is 27. Kg2. (Both the Rxe4 and the Kg2 ideas are addressed in my previous comment.)* **27. ... Black resigns.**

I didn't know computers could resign until right then, and I really wanted to finish the game. *White is winning, but not instantly: 27... Rg8 28. Qh5+ Nh6, and Black holds, if only for a while.*

Game 19: Older Players Can Be Deadly Tacticians, Too

If you've missed the right move in a position you deem important, make a note and return to it in several weeks. Thus, you'll learn, and remember, what you want to know and remember.

Good strategy is a foundation of our game, but tactics still reign supreme, as our next game illustrates.

Writes Tom Rogers:
I thoroughly enjoy your column each month in *Chess Life*, and am particularly encouraged by the numerous diagrams, allowing me to understand the comments without a board. It is a good exercise to visualize the moves between diagrams and try to recognize the threats as they develop.

The following game was played at a time control of Game/45 in a Westfield New Jersey Chess Club Quad tournament. As often occurs in lower-rated sections, the players in this game were 40 years apart in age. What is unusual about this tactically complex game is that the older player came out on top.

Caro-Kann
Exchange Variation [B13]
White: Teddy Katz (1521)
Black: Tom Rogers (1499)
Westfield Action Quads

1. e4 c6 2. d4 d5 3. exd5 cxd5

4. Bd3

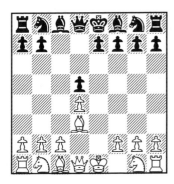

I love to see a diagram at least once every five moves, and in any important position, too. I try to do it in my books and articles. Still, extra diagrams make books bulkier, and articles longer.

4. ... Nf6 5. Bf4 Nc6 6. c3 Bg4 7. Nf3

Better is 7. Qb3!, transposing to the main line, as presented on page 394 in the **White Book.**

7. ... e6

Here 7... Bxf3 would be OK, keeping White's Queen from going to b3 (after 8. Qxf3).

8. Nbd2 Bd6

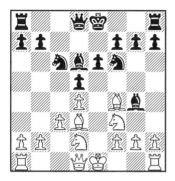

I was a bit hesitant with this move. I recalled it from other Caro-Kann variations, but it seems to offer to trade White's bad bishop for Black's good bishop. On the plus side, Black's position is less cramped after the trade.

I like 8. ... Bd6, while understanding Tom's hesitations. White's f4-bishop isn't "bad" at all. In particular, it keeps the black rook from b8, and from supporting the b7-pawn's "minority attack" march.

9. Bg5 0-0 10. Qc2

10. Qb3 is better. Black then gets tangled up a bit with 10... Qe7 to protect b7 and f6 at the same time. White can then try to win a pawn with 11. Bxf6 Qxf6 12. Qxb7.

No, 10. Qc2 is a good move, which forces ... h6 (see my comment to White's 12th move). If 10. Qb3, Rb8!, and then the thematic ... b7-b5.

10. ... h6 11. Bh4 Be7

I'd prefer 11. ... Rb8, and then ... b7-b5.

12. 0-0-0

A blunder, lining up King and Queen on the same file.

Even if not for ... Nb4, why castle into attack? After 12. h3, forcing 12. ... Bxf3 (not 12. ... Bh5 13. g4 — thanks to 10. ... h6) 13. Nxf3, followed by Qe2, 0-0, etc., White is slightly better, thanks to Black's uncalled-for retreat (11. ... Be7).

12. ... Nb4

Though this is not terribly difficult to find, I'm proud of this move and the tactical melee that follows. In past games, I would not have had the confidence to play such a move, and particularly not against a youngster with such a good reputation.

(Teddy is ranked 24th in the nation in the 9 and under age group.)

If 13. cxb4 Rc8. I have studied your entire **Comprehensive Chess Course**, and have worked through the sixth volume (**Chess**

Training Pocket Book: 300 Most Important Positions & Ideas) three times, recognizing more of the patterns each time. Currently, I am at about problem 700 of Fred Reinfeld's *1001 Winning Chess Sacrifices and Combinations.*

13. Qb1

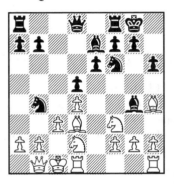

13. ... Nxd3+
A master might now play the subtle 13. ... Rc8; still 13. ... Nxd3 is winning, too.

14. Qxd3 Bf5

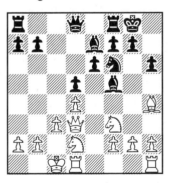

15. Qe2
15. Qb5 looks intriguing for White. It is not so much that the

Queen can cause a lot of trouble for Black, but she would prevent Black from causing trouble for White.
15. Qb5! may delay Black's assault, but only for a short time, e.g., 15. ... Qc8 and 16. ... a6, or even 15. ... a6!?

15. ... Qa5 16. a3

16. ... Qxa3
This is not a sacrifice, but it is another tactical shot to be proud of. If 17. bxa3 Bxa3 mate.
Very nice, but 16. ... Qxc3+, executing the same idea in a different fashion, wins instantly — mate in two.

17. Nb1 Qa2 18. Nfd2 Rfc8
White has defended well. Now the c3 square is threatened, since the b2 pawn is pinned, too.

19. Rhg1

> *When you see a good move, make a mental note and then look for a better one. (Unless you're in time pressure, of course).*

19. ... Ba3
Threatening 20... Qxb2 mate.
If 20. bxa3 Qc2 mate.
*Good, but 19. ... Ne4 was both
winning — and simple. When
winning, avoid unnecessary complications.*
20. Qb5 Rxc3+
This is a sacrifice, as I could
not see from here to the end.
White's reply is forced, and I did
see as far as 23... Qxb1+ and was
reasonably comfortable that material would come out close to
even and Black's king would be
in a somewhat safer position than
White's.
21. Nxc3 Rc8 22. Qb3

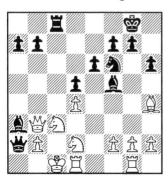

22. ... Qa1+
Fritz tells me I missed a
forced mate here: 22. ... Qxb2+
23. Qxb2 Rxc3 mate. Apparently,
I need to continue studying tactics!
*I missed it too! (Perhaps subconscious attachment to the
queen was the cause).*
23. Ndb1 Qxb1+ 24. Kd2

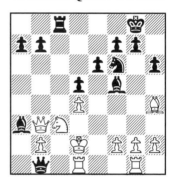

24. ... Qd3+
Again, Fritz points out that
24... Qxb2+ 25. Qxb2 Bxb2 is
winning.
*Yes, and does it in a simple,
safe manner. I would give a "?"
to 24. ... Qd3+.*
25. Ke1 Qc2

With two pawns for the exchange and running short on time, I decided that my best choice would be to head for the ending. **26. Qxc2 Bxc2 27. Rc1 Bxb2 28. Rxc2 Bxc3+ 29. Ke2 b5.**
Rejecting a natural pawn capture, 24. ... Qxb2+, on a prior move, Black is no longer better, and barely holds with 25. ... Qc2 26. Qxa3 Rxc3.
26. Qxb7
Heading for the ending was probably White's best chance, too. This move is a blunder and keeps Black's attacking chances alive.
26... Rc4
Fritz says that 26... Rxc3 is better, but at this point, I did not see the possibilities developing around e2, and so did not want to sacrifice more material to remove the defender. The tame 26... Rc4 allows White to launch a counterattack.
The point of 26. ... Rxc3: if 27. bxc3, then ... Qe4+ and ... Qxh4.
27. Bxf6 gxf6 28. g4 Bd3

Now the threat to e2 is clear and the wisdom of removing the c3 knight also.
29. g5
Fritz shows that White can hang on with 29. Rd2.
29... hxg5 30. Qb8+ Kg7 31. Qg3 Rxc3

White has no time to recapture due to ... Qe2 mate.
32. Qg4 Qxb2 33. f4
We are both in time trouble now, and White makes the final mistake, removing a defender of e3. h4 is better.
Anyway Black is winning: 33. ... Bb4!.
33... Bf5 34. Qh5 Re3+ 35. Kf1 Bh3+
One last tactical shot, deflecting the queen.
36. Qxh3 Qe2, mate.

Game 20:
A Student Applies Coach's Principles

The game below has most of the elements that make chess so exciting: a sharp, unorthodox opening, where Black soon wrestled the initiative; "the more developed side must attack" rule-of-thumb in action; a not-so-obvious sacrifice; a missed opportunity to win in one move, followed by good realization-of-advantage technique and a well-deserved victory.

Also interesting — to me and for you, readers, (I hope) is the thought-process which led Gary Zintgraff to his (mostly correct; one incorrect move is equally revealing) decisions. Gary's game was published already, in the November 2003 issue of the *San Antonio Chess Club News*, with in-depth comments by Selby Anderson, some of which I've used. Writes Gary:

———

This game was important to me because the same opponent beat me with the same opening the prior month in a tournament. It also used many of the principles that NM Jim Gallagher used to teach to us, such as: (1) Development and king safety should precede your attack; (2) No pawn captures — no open lines; no open lines — no attack; (3) And the old Steinitz dictum that you

are "obligated" to attack when you are much better developed, and if you don't you may end up worse.

———

Ruy Lopez [C63]
Schliemann Defense
White: Juan Carrizales (1762)
Black: Gary Zintgraff (1752)

1. e4 e5 2. Nf3 Nc6 3. Bb5 f5

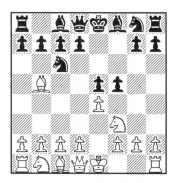

4. Bxc6
The moves 4. Nc3 (the strongest), 4. d4, and 4. d3 (the safest) are main lines. Using 4. Bxc6 is good mostly if you want a draw — or know for sure that your opponent doesn't.
4. ... dxc6 5. 0-0?!
Stronger is 5. exf5 e4 6. Qe2 Qe7 7. Nd4 Qe5 and a forced repetition follows: 8. Nf3! Qe7!, etc., or to avoid the draw, 5. Nc3.
5. ... fxe4 6. Nxe5

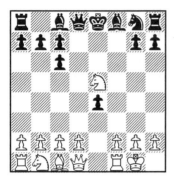

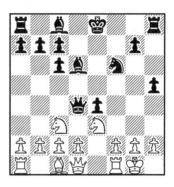

6. ... Qd4!
The right choice, much stronger than 6. ... Nf6 7. d4=. Zintgraff played 6. ... Nf6 in an earlier game, which he lost.
7. Ng4
Black need not fear 7. Qh5+ g6 8. Nxg6 hxg6 9. Qxg6+ Kd8 10. d3 Bd6, with decisive advantage.
7. ... h5

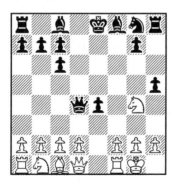

This is not a weakness, but a prelude to attack.
8. Ne3 Nf6 9. Nc3 Bd6

10. g3?
White's 10. g3? weakened the king's field and also gave Black a free developing move with 10. ... Bh3. Now I had five pieces developed to his three, so I came out of the opening fairly well as Black. Also his king was in a coffin corner dominated by my light square bishop.

White was afraid of possible sacs on h2, but the cure is worse than the disease. White's best defense was developing 10. d3, leaving Black a pleasant choice between a much better ending (10. ... exd3) and a strong attack (10. ... Qe5 or 10. ... Bg4).
10. ... Bh3 11. Ne2 Qc5 12. Re1 0-0-0 13. d3 exd3 14. cxd3

14. ... Ng4
The attack begins in earnest.
15. Nxg4 hxg4
The recapture 15. ... hxg4 opened the h-file and developed my Rh8 without even moving it! Now the development was five pieces to two. There had to be something there.
16. Nc3

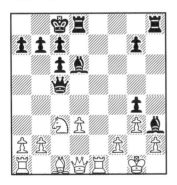

Black was threatening 16. ... Qd5.
16. ... Bxg3!!
The bishop sac at 16. ... g3 just looked right immediately after White played 16. Nc3 to keep my queen off the long diag-

onal. After a quick initial assessment of three candidate moves (16. ... Bxg3 followed by 17. ... Qh5; 16. ... Qh5; or 16. ... Qf5) the sac looked good even if he didn't take the bishop and instead played 17. Be3? Bxh2+; or 17. Ne4? Bxh2+; or 17. d4? Bxf2+ 18. Kxf2 Rxd4. My real worry was if he played what I thought was the best move, 17. hxg3 Qh5 18. Re4!.

After 18. Re4!

I burned 20 minutes looking for some way to continue the attack or get material back and almost gave up the sac idea, preferring the safer 16. ... Qf5 until I saw that 18. ... Kb8 would allow me to still pull off my desired follow-up ... Bg2! sac without the white queen taking at g4 with check! That settled it. The first bishop sac had to go in.

As it turned out, White played 18. Be3?, which allowed me to continue with my original plan of 18. ... Bg2!. White had to give up his queen to avoid mate.

The thought process on finding 18. ... Kb8 (first identifying the problem, then solving it) is very illuminating.
17. hxg3 Qh5

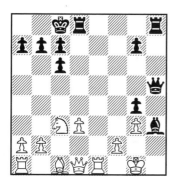

18. Be3?
*This loses quickly and simply,
but White is lost anyway.*
**18. ... Bg2! 19. Qxg4+ Qxg4
20. Kxg2**

20. ... Rdf8
*Gary looked at 20. ... Rh2+
21. Kxh2 Qf3 22. any Rh8+, but
rejected it because of 22. Bg5.*
21. f4 Qh3+?
I "forgot or had chess blind-
ness" about ... Rh2+ followed by
22. ... Qf3 for a quick finish. I
had looked at it and rejected it as
faulty the move before. Once
White played 21. f4, blocking his
dark squared bishop, it would

have worked.
*This is another important ob-
servation, showing how mistakes
often are made (pre-existing vision). The remedy: re-examine a
position after every move made
on board, don't rely on your earlier mental analysis alone.*
**22. Kf2 Qh2+ 23. Kf3 Qh5+
24. Kg2 Qh3+**
I just got cautious with the
material advantage and chose not
to take the b-pawn since Bd4
looked worrisome.
25. Kf3 g5

26. Bf2
*Tougher resistance is offered
by 26. Ne4 gxf4 27. Bxf4, but
Black makes inroads with 27. ...
Rh4! (with the idea ... Rxf4), as
shown by Selby Anderson.*
**26. ... Rxf4+ 27. Ke3 Re8+
28. Ne4 Rff8**

29. Kd2?
Loses instantly.
29. ... Rxe4, and White resigns.

Game 21: The Perpetual (Attack)

An inaccuracy in a won position may allow a spectacular escape —
for instance, by a perpetual check.
Here's an example from the Fischer era.

Jack Stillman submitted a remarkable game — played long ago — and good notes. We'll see winning-the-queen-turned-bad and a Houdini-like escape. Writes Mr. Stillman:

I am 83 years old and playing chess. I enjoy playing against my Mephisto computer even though it beats me most of the time. I'm unrated — after year 1975, I didn't play chess for many years.

Thirty-seven years ago, when I was a member of the Downey Chess Club, I played a game against Mr. Bicknell, an Expert. I don't remember his first name. After so many years, I don't remember my exact rating, but I believe it was in the 1500-1600 range.

I selected the following game because of the mistakes — made by both players — resulting in a surprising finish. I had the white pieces; my opponent played Alekhine's Defense.

Alekhine's Defense,
Four Pawns Attack [B03]
White: Jack Stillman
Black: Mr. Bicknell
Downey Chess Club, 1971

1. e4 Nf6 2. e5 Nd5

3. c4 Nb6 4. d4 d6 5. f4

I played the Four Pawns Attack, thinking that it was the most aggressive variation.

Four Pawns Attack indeed is very aggressive. On the negative side (for White) Black has a choice of a dozen defenses, all very sharp, at least two or three leading to dynamic equality. Thus, most players prefer to play 3. d4 d6 4. Nf3 (after 1. e4 Nf6 2. e5 Nd5), a so-called classical line, with a small edge for White.

5. ... dxe5 6. fxe5 Nc6

7. Be3
I didn't want to play 7. Nf3 because of 7. ... Bg4, pinning my knight.
7. ... Bf5 8. Nc3 e6 9. Nf3

9. ... Be7
If Black wanted to castle long, he should have done it without playing 9. ... Be7: 9. ... Qd7 and 10. ... 0-0-0.
10. Be2 Qd7
Now, the best for Black was 10. ... 0-0, followed by 11. ... f6, with equality.
11. 0-0 0-0-0

Castling queenside tells me that he'll attack on the kingside. I should attack on the queenside.
12. a4
An interesting plan. Ernst Gruenfeld long ago recommended here 12. d5, with an edge.
12. ... a5 13. Qb3
I wanted to move a pawn to d5, attacking the b6 knight.
I think d4-d5 was even stronger here (on Move 13) than a move ago, as after, say, 13. ... exd5 14. Bxb6

After
14. Bxb6

Black would have to capture on b6 with his c- (not a-)pawn, leaving White with a great pawn center (after 15. cxd5).
13. ... Nb4

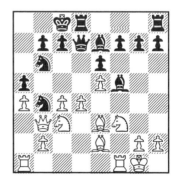

14. Ne1 Bg6 15. Rd1 Qc6?

16. c5
Because winning the queen, as in the game, isn't so good for White as it initially appears, perhaps White should have delayed the trapping by playing first, for instance, 16. Rd2.
16. ... N6d5 17. Bb5!
I trapped his queen, but the game isn't over.
The exclam doesn't belong here.
17. ... Nxe3 18. Bxc6 Nxc6

19. Nf3?
A blunder! I think I should have played Rd2.
After 19. Rd2, the simple 19.

... Nxf1 20. Kxf1 Nxd4 (or 20. ... Bxc5) favors Black, who soon will be ahead in material. I'd prefer 19. Nb5 Nxd1 20. Nf3!, with chances for both sides.
19. ... Bc2

*Now Black gets **two** Exchanges.*
20. Qb5 Bxd1 21. Nxd1 Nxf1 22. Kxf1 Nxd4 23. Nxd4 Rxd4

24. Nc3
White should have tried here 24. c6, hoping for 24. ... Rxd1+? 25. Ke2. Yes, Black is much better after 24. ... bxc6, but his road to victory after the uninspired 24. Nc3 is easier.

24. ... c6 25. Qxa5 R8d8 26.
Qa8+

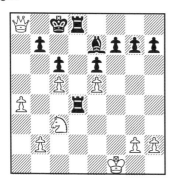

*Relatively better is 26. b4 —
as played two moves later. Driving Black's king to b8 only makes
White's position even worse.*
**26. ... Kc7 27. Qa5+ Kb8 28.
b4 Rc4 29. Ne2 Rd1+ 30. Kf2**

At this point, I thought I had a
lost game. Black had a definite
material advantage and sounder
position. However, after searching further I discovered that I
could draw by perpetual check.
**33. Nxc6+ bxc6 34. Qb6+
Kc8 35. Qxc6+**

30. ... Rb1
There is no way I can defend
the b-pawn.
*The easiest win was after 30.
... Bd8! In a won position, be diligent. Stay alert for the kill!*
31. b5? Rxc5??
Black missed a win! Instead,
31. ... Bxc5+.
32. Nd4 Rd5

35. ... Kd8 36. Qa8+ draw.

Overlooking just one move
can be disastrous. I was fortunate
to get a draw.
*Fortunate, but deserving —
as indicated by "searching further" in Jack's comment to 32. ...
Rd5.*

Game 22: Press On!

Nobody ever won by resigning — Savielly Tartakower

There is a saying that complements that of Tartakower above, "the most difficult task is to win a won position." That expression owes a lot to tenacious folks like Vietnam veteran Jim Dautremont, now a fresh-minted author of an interesting (perhaps "amazing" is better word) chess book, *Chess Play from A to Z*. Writes Jim:

Granted, there is no substitute for basic intelligence in chess; but to be a successful chessplayer one must possess several additional personal characteristics — one of which is tenacity. As we soldiers were wont to say in Vietnam, "Press on!" The following rated game, played online, gives a good example, I think, of how hanging tough in the face of adversity can pay off in chess — as in life.

Slav Defense [D17]
White: WimpB (1443)
Black: Jim Dautremont (1403)
2009
Time Control: 2 minutes per game plus 8-second increments

**1. d4 c6 2. c4 d5 3. Nf3 Nf6
4. Nc3 dxc4 5. a4 Bf5 6. Ne5**

Nbd7

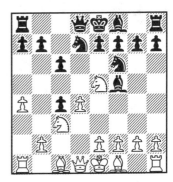

7. Nxc4 Nd5 8. Bg5 Nxc3 9. bxc3 h6??

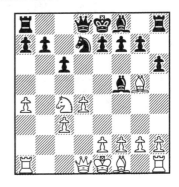

Just after I made this move, I groaned so loudly that I scared my trusty dog Lucy! I was tempted to give up on the spot. But I decided to punish myself for my inattention, continuing on for a while against all odds.

10. Nd6+ exd6 11. Bxd8 Rxd8

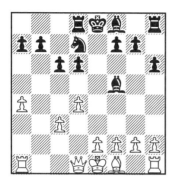

12. d5

Better to build up White's decisive advantage by simple, and strong, means — 12. e3 and 13. Bd3. After receiving such a gift, don't relax! A little self-indulgence now may cost you a lot of troubles later.

12. ... c5 13. g3 g6

I'd prefer to play 13. ... Be7, and then ... Bf6.

14. h3 (*14. Bg2! — LA*)
14. ... g5 (*14. ... Bg7! — LA*)
15. Qc1 Bg7 16. Ra2 Ne5 17. Qb2

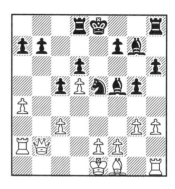

17. ... b6

Tenacity should include alertness. Black could get back in the game by 17. ... Be4, winning (among other goodies) the d5-pawn.

18. g4

White is asking for ... Be4 — in vain.

18. ... Bg6

Now I have the Horwitz bishops and a pretty good knight.

19. Qb5+ Rd7 20. a5 0-0

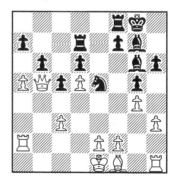

My king is now tucked away with some good protection, and I am beginning to feel just a bit more sanguine about my position. Thought I, "My opponent is no grandmaster, so I might play on to see what develops."

21. Ra1

A mysterious move to me, even now! Maybe with the intent of backing up the white c-pawn?

21. ... Re7

Naturally putting my rook on the half-open file and X-raying the white king.

22. axb6 axb6 23. Qxb6

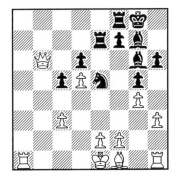

23. ... Nc4

Another missed opportunity. Why not 23. ... Nd3+, as after 24. Kd2 Nxf2, the d6 pawn is taboo (25. Qxd6? Ne4+)?

24. Qb3 Ne5 25. Bg2

After the loss of time (Ne5-c4 and back) and several opportunities (listed above) Black is back to square one, to where he was after his ninth move blunder.

25. ... Rfe8

Black should play here 25. ... Nd3+ 26. Kf1 Rfe8, achieving the position which happened in the game. See diagram, bottom right.

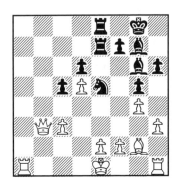

26. Kf1?!

Another mystery move that seems to give me some chances,. I expected White to castle.

Of course!

26. ... Nd3!

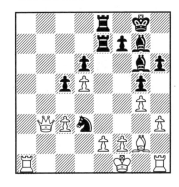

This was the chance I was hoping for — a swindle opportunity! And greedy White then proceeded to fall into my little trap. Greed is a cardinal sin in chess.

27. exd3 Bxd3+ 28. Kg1 Re1+ 29. Rxe1 Rxe1+ 30. Bf1

Rather better than 30. Kh2?? because of 30. ... Be5+ with mate to follow.

30. ... Bxf1 31. Qb8+

Getting the queen off of the b3 square.

31. ... Kh7 32. f4

If 32. Qxd6, then Bxh3+ 33. Kh2 Be5+ 34. Qxe5 Rxe5 35. Kxh3 Rxd5, with an easily-won endgame for Black.

32. ... Bc4+

Not winning the queen because of White's perspicacious 31st move.

33. Kh2 Re2+ 34. Kg3 gxf4+

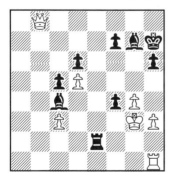

Wow! Now White must not take that bodacious f-pawn, because if 35. Kxf4, then comes the *Zwischenzug* 35. ... Bxd5!,

After 35. ... Bxd5!

leaving White with no saving move (*e.g.*, if 36. Rf1, then Be5+ 37. Kf5 Be4 mate; and if 36. Qxd6, then Bxh1 *(36. ... Be5+! — L.A.)* 37. Qxc5 Re4+, etc.

But 36. Qb1+ saves White — a draw by repetition. Thus, after 35. Kxf4, Black's best try to avoid a draw is 35. ... Be5+ 36. Kf3 Rc2.

35. Kf3 Be5

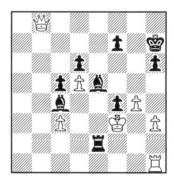

There will be a material equality (bishop pair and two pawns for a queen) very soon, while White's king and the remaining pawns are much more vulnerable than their Black counterparts. Black is clearly better.

36. Rc1 Re3+ 37. Kf2 Re2+

A time-trouble move — asking White, by implication, if he

wants a draw by repetition
38. Kg1?!

White declines the possibility of a draw.

38. ... f3!

Creating a "Little Bishop".

39. Qb1+ Kg7 40. Rf1 Rg2+ 41. Kh1 Rg3!

Declining White's proffered exchange sacrifice, I instinctively conclude that I *must* have something better here.

Of course, 41. ... Bxf1 42. Qxf1 Rh2+ 43. Kg1 f2+ leaves Black with an extra bishop and a very easy win.

42. Rc1 Rxh3+ 43. Kg1

Bxd5 44. Rd1 Be6 45. Qb2 Rg3+

Now not 46. Kf2, 46. Kh2, or 46. Kf1 because the queen would perish. So White's only choice is:

46. Kh1 Bxg4

To paraphrase Senator Everett Dirksen of Illinois, "A pawn here, a pawn there — pretty soon you're talking real material!"

47. Ra1 Rg2

48. Qxg2 fxg2+, with a simple winning endgame for Black.

This come-from-behind victory serves as a reminder to all chessplayers that tenacity (*i.e.,* scrappiness) is a valuable characteristic for any player.

Part V
Tactics

Game 23: Shock And Awe Out Of The Blue Sky

Sometimes even apparently dull positions contain hidden tactical explosives. Be alert, and if opportunity knocks, be ready to open the door!

Shannon Fox marked his letter to me "When opportunity knocks". When his opportunity did knock, Shannon was ready.

I've read several of your books and my favorite is *Chess Openings for Black Explained*. I've used that book to help me with ideas and to build confidence when playing against the most popular opening lines as Black. The following game I played at the US Air Force Academy in Colorado Springs on Dec. 20th, 2008, utilizing some of the book's positional ideas. My opponent is Tony Telinbacco, rated 1826, whom I previously played in the same venue earlier this Fall. In our prior match, Tony played a very sound conservative game winning a pawn in the middlegame and then grinding me through a long endgame with him eventually winning.

In our second game, I had a fairly good idea of what to expect so I decided to stick with familiar lines and try to avoid the mistakes from our prior match.

Queen's Indian Defense [A47]
White: Tony Telinbacco (1826)
Black: Shannon Fox (1630)
US Air Force Academy Quads, 2008

1. d4 Nf6 2. Nf3 b6

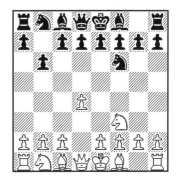

In the above-noted repertoire book, the authors suggest 2. ... e6, ready to meet 3. c4 with 3. ... Bb4+, the Bogo-Indian. But 2. ... b6 is, of course, as good as 2. ... e6.

3. Nbd2 Bb7

I'm not playing in normal move order here for the Nimzo-Indian but it seems to be okay.

4. e3 e6 5. Bd3

5. ... Be7

I'd prefer 5. ... c5, limiting White's options.

6. 0-0 d6

Instead of d6, I quite often play c5 and put pressure on White's center. With ... d6 I'm a bit passive but it does allow for the logical development of the knight from b8 to d7 with additional support for e5.

As in the note above, I'd prefer 6. ... c5. I think that after 6. ... d6 7. e4 White is a little better.

7. b3 0-0 8. Bb2 Nbd7

9. e4 c5

Fritz prefers ... d5 for Black

instead of ... c5. My idea, of course, is to challenge the center while keeping a potential line open for the light-squared bishop. The time control in this Quad was G60 with a five second delay and as a result, I was keeping my opening moves in the 1-3 minute range so, I didn't look very long at the alternate d5 move before I chose c5.

The point of the transformational 9. ... d5 is to meet 10. e5 with 10. ... Ne4.

10. e5 dxe5 11. dxe5 Nd5

I was surprised at c5 by White because it strengthened Black's light-square bishop and it seemed a bit premature to lose the tension in the center.

The black and white light-square bishops neutralize each other, while White's space advantage gives him the overall edge.

12. Be4 Qc7

I spent a fair amount of time before playing Qc7 to ensure that the knight on d5 had an active square to eventually reach if White booted it with 13. c4 Nf4 and possibly on to ... Ng6. The positional consequence that I did not give enough consideration to was allowing White to exchange off Black's good bishop, which left Black with a less active bishop on e7. This is the type of mistake that I often make when playing higher rated players. I end up with equal material but bad pieces with not much initiative.

That's why I didn't like allowing White to play e5 to begin with.

13. Qe2 Nf4 14. Qe3 Ng6 15.Bxb7 Qxb7

16. Rad1 b5

With ... b5, I'm looking for more space on the queenside to allow the black knight to move to b6 and possibly d5.

17. Ne4 Rfd8

18. Nd6

As the knight can't be maintained there, I'd prefer to double the white rooks over the d-file, tying up Black's forces. In particular, the c5-pawn needs protection.

18. ... Qc6 19. c4 bxc4

I'm a bit concerned about Black's pawn on c5 with no pawn support, but I have a lot of piece protection for c5 .

20. Nxc4 Nb6

I finally get my knight to b6 and the position is about equal or maybe a slight advantage for White. Considering I'm a 200 rating point underdog I'm feeling a bit more confident at this point in the game. Black's pieces are on fairly active squares and I want to continue with my idea of getting the knight to d5.

21. Nxb6

White quickly exchanges off the knight and prevents the nice post on d5.

I'd do almost anything to prevent Black's axb6 recapture! (Two benefits for Black: capturing toward the center, and reconnecting pawns.) Stronger, for instance, is 21. Rc1 with a small edge for White.

21. ... axb6 22. Rxd8+ Rxd8

Exchanging the rooks seems to favor Black slightly; I'm starting to feel better about my position. I think White will try to post his knight on d6 which will be tough to boot and dangerous to exchange with Black's bishop on e7. I'm looking for a way to continue to push my queenside pawns and get additional play on that side of the board.

23. Qe2 Nf4

White makes an inferior queen move giving me a tempo and now I get the knight to f4 and on to d5!

24. Qc4

24. ... Nd5

Better is 24. ... Nd3, followed by 25. ... b5 and then ... c4. Black's knight is even better placed on d3 (compared to d5). If 25. Nd4, then 25. ... Qe4.

25. Nd4 (? — L.A.) Qa8

I spent additional time to come up with Qa8. I want to keep the queen on the a8-h1 diagonal with the g2 target. Plus, I gain a bit more initiative because White needs to consider the threat to the pawn on a2.

26. Nc2

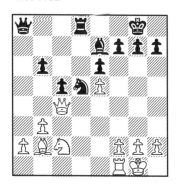

26. ... Qb7

Oops, I realize that I need the

rook on a8 so, it turns out that I wasted a move and should have played Qb7 a move earlier. I'm not overly concerned though, because White hasn't got much counterplay at this point. *I guess at this moment Shannon wasn't employing Fritz's help in annotating the game. The move 26. ... Qxa2 simply wins a pawn (if 27. Ba3, then 27. ... b5, untrapping the black queen).*

27. a4 Rb8 28. Na3 Rd8

I didn't see White playing Na3, stopping my attack with the hopeful ... b5 pawn push, so I moved the rook back to d-file again, looking for an active square and possibly to break into White's position.

29. Rd1 Rd7

I was a bit uneasy with Rd7 but I wanted to avoid a future rook exchange with White getting a check if I left the rook on d8. *29. ... Rd7 is a superb move which sets up many threats, and many traps,. For example, any* *knight move, or bishop move, is refuted by 30. ... Nf4, winning; the same 30. ... Nf4 wins after 30. Rd3 or 30. Qc1, while 30. Rd2 loses to 30. ... Ne3. To survive, White should play defense and make concessions — for example 30. Re1.*

30. Qd3

When White played Qd3 I thought that he had made a strong/logical move and proved that my rook in fact had been badly placed on d7 with his queen/rook battery. Then I noticed the discovered attack with my knight jumping to f4 and the mate threat on g2. I had plenty of time on my clock so I re-examined the position double checking that I wasn't sacrificing my rook for nothing. Yep, the rook was correctly placed on the seventh rank.

31. ... Nf4!

At first, Tony looked at this move with disbelief and it definitely took him by surprise. White is totally lost and if White tries Qf1 he ends up losing both his queen and rook. Looking back at this game, it reaffirms that if you have a tactical threat hold on to it and make your opponent deal with it; don't undo a strong tactical position willingly. In this case, not moving the black queen from the a8-h1 and when opportunity knocks, be ready to open the door!

White resigns.

Let's give also a well-deserved credit to the subtle 29. ... Rd7, and hurrah for our aces!

Game 24: When Fortune Smiles on You, Be Ready!

Playing the board is perhaps the most important lesson the class player can learn. In this game, a Class C player takes advantage of an IM who perhaps momentarily forgot that lesson.

You are a C-player playing an IM in a simul. You navigated well through an unknown opening and, on Move 26, achieved a position you felt you "couldn't lose."

Being up an Exchange for a pawn, you want to get the queens off the board, and now you see an opportunity to do just that.

An Opportunity Seized

After 31. c3

So, you play 31. ... Qd6, simultaneously offering the queen trade and attacking the d3-pawn. Your opponent protects the pawn with a natural 32. Rf3, and now the endgame, perhaps a won endgame (32. ... Qxf6 33. gxf6 Rb8) is within your grasp. So, do you:

a) quickly and confidently follow your original intent and exchange queens, or

b) make a mental note that 32. ... Qxf6 is both possible and good for you, and look for a better

move (which may or may not exist)?

Greg Roudebush sought and found a better move — he trapped the White queen, forcing a resignation. Writes Greg:

I recently played in a simul at our chess club. The reason I feel I won this game is that the IM in question knew I was a 1440 player and played more relaxed against me than he would against a higher-rated opponent. I know I play more relaxed when facing someone 300 points lower than me. I don't condone that, for when we play more relaxed, that's when we get ourselves into trouble. I believe Bobby Fischer said that when facing an opponent, no matter what his rating, he always faced them as if they were a GM.

This game is instructional for it shows that if the stronger player does relax his play and the weaker player plays his hardest, the weaker player can pounce on the slightest mistake.

Of course, in a simul, the participant does have a slight advantage as the giver is playing so many games at once and mistakes are apt to happen.

I know I have a long way to go before my play gets to the level of an IM, but on this particular day, the game turned my way. It is a game that I will always remember and treasure as a "C" player.

A few comments. As a rule, you should search for the best move, "play the board" — as in the case of Fischer assuming that his opponent is a GM. Only in some (rare) situations do you consider your opponent's rating: for instance, you may choose to play an unclear position against a weaker, or even equal, opponent — but force a draw by a perpetual check against someone 200 points higher. And IM Taylor blundered (I guess) not because he underestimated his opponent, but of necessity to play fast and end the simul on time.

Bird's Opening [A03]
White: Tim Taylor (2375)
Black: Greg Roudebush (1440)
Los Angeles Chess Club Simul, 2006

1. f4 d5
Little did I know, this is book and is the first move in the Dutch Variation in the Bird System.

It's good for a chessplayer to know "a little about all" openings, and a lot about openings

you play.
2. Nf3 Bf5
I didn't know Bg4 was book and I felt it was important to get my bishop out, so I put it on a safe square.

Still, Greg's choice is logical and good.
3. e3 Nf6 4. Be2

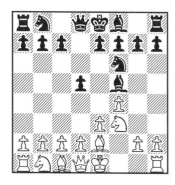

4. ... c5 5. 0-0 Nc6 6. Bb5
Black could avoid these problems by playing first 4. ... e6, 5. ... Be7, and 6. ... 0-0, and only then ... c5.
6. ... e6 7. Bxc6+ bxc6 8. b3 Bd6

A better move would have

been 8. ... Be7.

True, as it allows eventual regrouping with ... Nd7 and ... Bf6.

9. Bb2

I wasn't happy about seeing his bishop on b2 and since my queenside was open, I knew I had to castle kingside and he could open it up if I moved the knight.

9. ... 0-0 10. Nc3

I didn't see any potential threats from his knight on c3. I figured he would develop it to e2 and expand on the queenside.

10. ... Re8

My plan, whether it was wise or not, was to somehow neutralize his b2 bishop.

11. Na4

11. ... Bg4 12. Qe1 Be7

I decided to protect my knight and try to figure out a way to expand on the queenside.

Perhaps Black's best defense here is 12. ... Bxf3 13. Rxf3 Nd7, planning 14. ... e5.

13. Qg3

I'd prefer 13. Ne5!, with dangerous attacking possibilities.

13. ... h5

I didn't see ... h7-h5 as a good move or a bad move, but I knew I could move the knight and not lose the bishop.

14. Ng5

Here, again, I'd prefer 14. Ne5.

14. ... d4

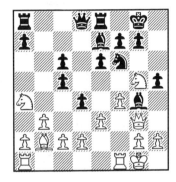

My attempt to block the a1-h8 diagonal.

15. e4 Be2

An excellent move, activating the otherwise dangerously exposed bishop.

16. Rfe1 Bb5

The knight has no good square to move to and I could create a weakness and try to exploit it.

Indeed. The roles have been reversed — now Black is better.

17. Qh4

If e4-e5 was coming, I would have to move the knight and lose the pawn. Not liking that, I protected the pawn.

Perhaps 17. d3 was stronger. White will lose tempi moving his

queen back and forth.
17. ... g6 18. d3

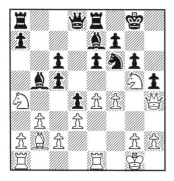

I wanted to take advantage of his pinned knight when I moved mine. I didn't know if it would have been better to move my knight to h7 or to g4. I considered both, and I'm honestly not sure which would have been the better move. I moved Ng4 to keep it active, and I saw the knight potentially going to c2.

True. The choice is not easy. I'd choose 18. ... Nh7, threatening to win a pawn.

18. ... Ng4 19. Qg3 Bxg5 20. fxg5 Bxa4 21. bxa4 c5

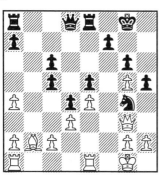

22. h3

Stronger was 22. Bc1, followed by 23. h3.

22. ... Ne3 23. Rxe3

I will admit I was surprised to see the exchange on e3.

This may be a case of rashness, based on underestimating the opponent. White should first defend the c2-pawn, and then play Bc1, with approximate equality.

23. ... dxe3 24. Qxe3 Qa5 25. Rf1 Rab8 26. Ba1

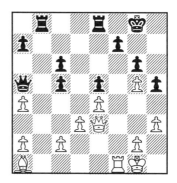

This is where I felt I could not lose, unless I really played bad. I felt the worst I could do would be to draw.

26. ... Qxa4 27. Qxc5 Qb5

I knew he could take a7 with his queen but I would force the queens off the board with Qb6+.

Still, this was White's best. White would have very good chances for a draw — but very little chance for a win, and that's why the natural 28. Qxa7 was perhaps rejected.

28. Qd6

He didn't want to trade queens and his move Qf6 could cause things to get nasty. I still wanted to get the queens off the board, so I did my best to position myself to do that.

28. ... Rbd8

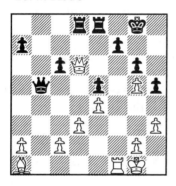

29. Qf6 Qc5+ 30. Kh1
Better was 30. Kh2, as in some lines the black rook comes to b1 with a check.

30. ... Rd7 31. c3
Since he prevented me from taking the pawn on c2, I offered a queen trade again and threatened the pawn on d3.

We're back to our first diagram.

31. ... Qd6 32. Rf3
With Rf3?? he took away any escape for his queen and I promptly took advantage of it.

A blunder, but even after the best 32. Qxd6 Rxd6 33. Rd1 c5!, Black should win.

32. ... Re6, White resigns.
When he came around to my board and saw his queen trapped,

he resigned. This game goes to show that even "C" players shine every once in a while.

Keep a Poker Face!

White to Move

This position happened in a game played by Michael Graves. His higher-rated opponent just grabbed the white bishop on b4, relying on the c-file pin. Michael, however, foresaw it and replied with ...

25. Re8+
Deflection!

25. ... Kg7

Michael says: I did not anticipate this reply and panicked in the face of the unexpected. I figured that my opponent would take the rook, after which I would take his queen. My gut reaction was to trade rooks on c8, but my opponent gave a heavy sigh after his move, and left the table. This is the only reason I looked harder and found the correct play! (Neither 25. ... Qf8 nor 25. ... Rxe8 solves his problem any better than the move he chose.)

Very important! When surprised — pleasantly or not — the gut reaction always should be to look harder, and think longer (unless you're running out of time, of course).

26. cxb4 Rxc2

The move 26. ... Rxe8

After 26. ... Rxe8

is countered by 27. Qc7.

Any reasonable 27th move preserved White's big edge. Still

— unlike in a game, after 26. ... Rxc2 — White's road to victory would be far from obvious.

27. Rxa8

27. ... Rxf2 28. Rxa7, Black resigns.

This game taught me a few good lessons: (1) Do not be intimidated by a higher-rated opponent — play as you would against an equal opponent; (2) Do not express your realization that you just made an error — doing so will just make your opponent look for your mistake; (3) A surprise move by your opponent may be surprising simply because it does not work.

Good lessons indeed.

Game 25: Turning the Tables— Pin Becomes Discovered Attack

Tactical alertness usually trumps everything else. A sudden move by a pinned piece — exposing a queen while attacking the "pinner" — is easy to overlook.

Ten-year-old Nicolo Gelb writes:

There was a very unusual situation for this game. I was playing in a five-round scholastic grade-level tournament (you only play people in your grade) with Swiss-system pairings and a G/30 sudden death time control. The tournament was using N.W.S.R.S. rating system. Surprisingly, going into the last game, my opponent and I were a full point ahead of the other fifth-graders, which very rarely happens at that type of scholastic tournament. I knew that I would probably have better tiebreaks than my opponent would, but I was playing for a win anyway. I knew a draw would make me happy, too.

Nimzo-Indian Defense [E34]
White: James Colasurdo
(NWSRS 1412)
Black: Nicolo Gelb
(NWSRS 1403)

1. d4 Nf6 2.c4 e6 3. Nc3 Bb4 4. Qc2 d5 5. Bg5

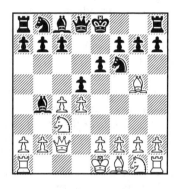

5. ... Nbd7
I don't know very much theory in the Nimzo-Indian Defense, so I was just following my intuition. I wanted to develop my light-squared bishop as effectively as possible and I also decided not to trade my bishop on b4 until he wasted a tempo with a3. My current goal was to get a firm grip on the center.

More common here is 5. ... dxc4 or 5. ... c5, both leading to equality. But 5. ... Nbd7 is also OK.

6. e3 b6
Here I was trying to activate my light squared bishop with a fianchetto, and support a central break-through with c5.

Good plan, wrong execution. White achieved an edge with 7. cxd5 exd5 8. Bb5!

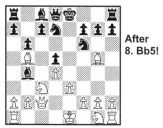

After 8. Bb5!

e.g., 8. ... h6 9. Bc6! Or 8. ... c5 9. Bc6 Rb8 10. Bf4, or 8. ... Bb7 9. Bxd7+.

7. Bd3

7. ... h6

Putting the question to the bishop on g5, and removing the target on h7 that his queen and light squared bishop are lined up against.

8. Bh4 Bb7 9. f3

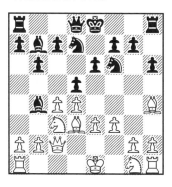

9. ... c5

White threatens to take over the center with e3-e4, so I counter with c7-c5.

Very good!

10. cxd5 exd5 11.a3 Bxc3+

After White wasted a tempo with a3, I finally decided to capture his knight.

12. Qxc3 Qe7

I completely missed White's next move

13. Bb5

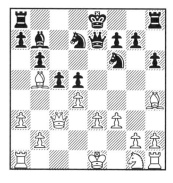

In this position, having both my knights pinned was very annoying. I didn't want to get doubled, isolated pawn on the f-file, so I decided to break one of the pins by exploiting the white queen's awkward placing. This also ends up trading down to an approximately equal endgame.

I'd add that solving the matter with 13. ... g5 would create a new set of problems (weak squares). Nicolo's solution is the best.

13. ... Ne4

If he takes my knight on e4, I play Qxh4+ followed by Qxe4,

and if he plays Bxe7 than I play Nxc3. Interpolating Bxd7+ and Kxd7 makes no major difference.

14. Bxd7+ Kxd7 15. Bxe7 Nxc3 16. bxc3 *(16. Bxc5!? Na4 — L.A.)* **16. ... Kxe7 17. Ne2**

17. ... Rac8
Trying to activate my rook and pressure his pawns.
The dust has settled. Black is fine.

18. 0-0
In such endgame positions, with central files closed, it is better to keep the king near the center.

At this point I decided to pin his knight with my bishop, and later trade the minor. This was because, although the position was mostly open, my bishop did not have any real targets that I could find.

18. ...Ba6 19. Rfe1

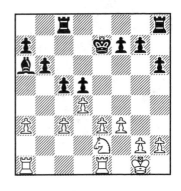

19. ... Rhe8
Activating my other rook.
I'd prefer the flexible 19. ... Kd6.

20. Rac1 Bxe2
I finally decided to trade off the minor pieces.

21. Rxe2 Kd6
Getting my king into the game.
Centralizing your king — very good!

22. Kf1

22. ... cxd4
Although this trade gives me an isolated d-pawn, the pawn is hard to get to, and it also gives

my rook a home on c4. Now my opponent has a backward c-pawn that's hard to defend, too.

Black's winning chances are better with all rooks on board. Thus, 22. ... Re7! was stronger — but this is a subtlety even a master may not find.

23. exd4 Rxe2 24. Kxe2 Rc4 25. Kd3 Ra4

Attacking his isolated a-pawn, so now both his pieces are temporarily tied down to defending weak pawns.

True, but only temporarily.

26. Ra1 Ke6

Here I wanted to break through on the kingside, while both his pieces are tied down.

Safer was to bring the rook back and to accept that the game should end in a draw. After 27. g4 g6 (see next diagram) White may get a somewhat better, albeit still drawish, game with 28. Kc2 and then Kb3, freeing his rook for real action. Remember: the rook is stronger than the king!

27. g4 g6

28. f4 f6 29. h4

29. ... Kd6, draw agreed.

Now I didn't see any favorable pawn breaks, and I was down on time, nine minutes versus fifteen minutes, so I offered a draw, and my opponent accepted. I ended up winning my section, on tiebreak.

White's last move allows Black such a break: 29. ... h5! Even if White finds the best move, 30. f5+, he's still on the defensive after 30. ... Kf7! (not 30. ... gxf5 31. gxh5!) Still, short on time, offering a draw was a good move.

Let's conclude this with a famous pin-turned-discovered-attack example, one which has to its credit many scalps, including some belonging to grandmasters. After

1. c4 e5 Nc3 Nc6 3. Nf3 f5 4. d4 e4 5. Bg5 Nf6 6. d5? exf3 7. dxc6 fxg2

the "normal" 8. cxd7+ has happened in many games. This is not surprising since it is so natural and appealing. (I observed it first-hand at Dubna, 1970: Razuvaev-Kupreichik). After the "unthinkable" 8. ... Nxd7 (pin turned discovered attack) White is completely lost. Thus, 8. Bxg2, accepting a pawn loss, was White's only choice.

Part VI
Strategy

Game 26: Capablanca's Formula

If your opponent's piece is caged, switch the action to another side of the board. You are now playing *de facto* a piece up.

In the position above, (Winter-Capablanca, 1919) Black won easily, while White's g3-bishop watched events helplessly. Ninety years later, Matt Cobb applied the same logical formula. Writes Mr. Cobb:

I recently played my first tournament in fifteen years. I have been studying chess for about a year and a half, since my oldest son showed an interest and began entering tournaments. He's now six, so I figured I'd get as much of a head start as possible, hoping to play with him for many years.

Among the things that I've learned that I didn't know fifteen years ago is that I need to have a plan of action at every point in the game. So when I put what I've learned to the test, it was quite rewarding to see a simple

plan play out against a player rated 400 points higher. I'm playing White against a very talented player, rated 1692 heading into the seventh grade!

Queen's Gambit Declined
[D37]
White: Matt Cobb (1293)
Black: Nick Moore (1692)
2010

1. d4 d5 2. c4 e6 3. Nf3 Be7 4. Bf4 Nf6 5. e3 0-0 6. Nc3 a6

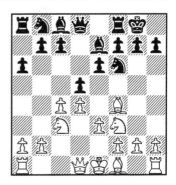

7. c5
The scholastic coaches in this area generally steer games toward open, tactical battles, so I chose 7. c5 as my best bet at bumping him out of his comfort zone.
7. ... Nbd7
Too passive. There are, in principle, three ways to counter c4-c5 in similar positions: un-

dermining with ... b6 (not effective here because White preserves his pawn chain: 7. ... b6 8. b4 a5 9. a3); breaking through in the center with ... e5, or playing ... Ne4 (but 7. ... Ne4 8. Nxe4 dxe4 9. Nd2 here favors White). Black's best here was the flexible 7. ... Nc6.

8. Bd3 b6 9. b4 a5 10. a3

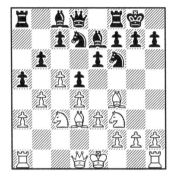

My efforts to this point are consistent with steering the game toward a positional battle. I've gained space, while not exchanging pawns or pieces. But I don't yet have a solid plan.

10. ... Ba6?

Since I knew what I wanted to do, I picked up on this error immediately, and a plan was formed. I will lock up the black queen's rook, knight, and bishop, hold e5, and move my pieces to kingside for the attack.

Spoken like Capablanca.

11. b5

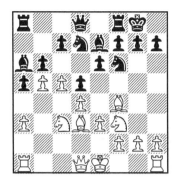

11. ... Bc8

Here was the last moment Black could (and should) get two pawns for a piece: 11. ... bxc5! 12. bxa6 c4 — albeit even here, White is winning!

12. c6 Nb8

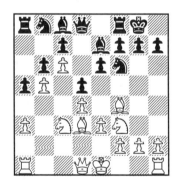

13. Be5

I would like to play a4 at some point, as well as castle, play Qc2, etc., but the plan calls for blockading e5 before my opponent can advance his e-pawn to that square. Everything else can wait.

Better 13. Ne5, followed by the attack with (g2)-g4-g5. Still

— it's an easy win.
13. ... Bd6 14. Qc2 h6 15. 0-0 Qe7 16. a4 Ng4 17. Rae1

17 ... Nxe5 18. Nxe5 Bxe5 19. dxe5
Black trades pieces, but this further stresses his need to free his queenside.
19. ... f6

Fighting for e5, but further compromising the king. At this point I'm spending a lot of time on calculations, but it's guided by my plan to hold e5 and move pieces to the kingside.
20. e4 d4 21. exf6

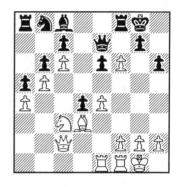

21. ... Qxf6
21 ... gxf6 would have given me trouble, but would also have further exposed Black's king.
Even if Black succeeds in freeing his bishop, his knight — and therefore his a8-rook — are completely cut off.
22. e5 Qg5 23. Ne2 Qxe5 24. Ng3 Qd6 25. Qe2

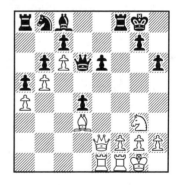

Black collected the e5 pawn, but took several tempos to do so. I was able to move my pieces on the right side of the board.
White finds a right winning plan — to bring his queen to e4, and then to h7.

25. ... Nxc6

What else? (See my comment to Black's 11th move.)

26. bxc6 Ra7?

Black wants to take the c6 pawn without the threat of the skewer Be4, but there are more important matters to attend to.

Material down and under mighty attack, Black is completely lost.

27. Qe4

Heavy loss of material is now unavoidable.

27. ... Qd5 28. Qh7+ Kf7 29. Bg6+ Kf6 30. Ne4+ Ke5

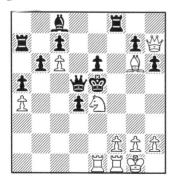

Here I missed mate in three: 31. f4+ Rxf4 32. Qxg7+ Rf6 33.

Qxf6 mate

The natural 31. Qxg7+ would also end the game in a few moves.

31. Nc3+ Kd6 32. Nxd5

and White went on to win the game.

With three pieces caged, Black had in this game very little chance of escape, especially as White understood the position, and his task, quite well.

Capablanca's formula performed its usual magic!

Another contributor,, Daren Dillinger, actually wrote a very good article, analyzing his game with Harold Kyriazi, of which I am using only the first part.

Sicilian Defense [B94]
White: Daren Dillinger
Black: Harold Kyriazi
10th Annual Jacksonville Open

1. e4 c5 2. Nf3 d6 3. d4 cxd4 4. Nxd4 Nf6 5. Nc3 a6 6. Bg5 Nbd7 7. f4

7. ... g6
More usual here is 7. ... e6.
8. Qf3 Bg7 9. 0-0-0 0-0 10. g4

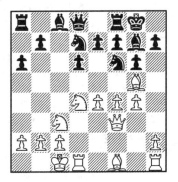

10. ... e5?!
This move is dubious for two reasons. (a) It will result in Black having a backward d-pawn, and (b) it will lead to blockaded pawns on the e5 and e4 squares, thereby hemming in his bishop.
11. Nde2 Qc7
11. ... exf4!
12. f5!

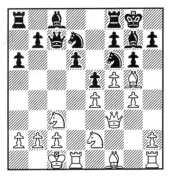

Now the effects of the last note become clear.
Yes, White has a clear strate-
gic (i.e., long-term) advantage ***after playing f4-f5***. *Thus, Black should have tried very hard to prevent it. I'd seriously consider (in a tournament game) or quickly play (in a blitz game) 11. ... exf4, even if it involves a pawn sacrifice.*
12. ... b5 13. Ng3

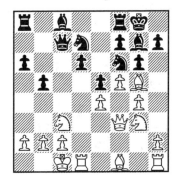

Better is 13. a3, as White played on the next move.
13. ... Bb7
Why not 13. ... b4! and only then ... Bb7, with counterplay?
14. a3

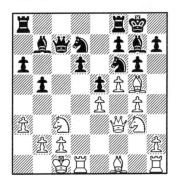

14. ... Rac8
What can Black do to stop the

coming avalanche? Perhaps better was 14., ... Rfc8, preparing for ... Nf6-e8 and, if needed, ... f7-f6.

15. h4

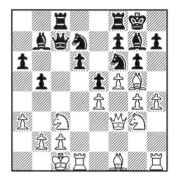

15. ... Nb6

Again, I'd prefer other concessions, anything to stop White's pawns coming to g5 and f6. Thus: 15. ... h6!?

16. Bxf6 Bxf6 17. g5 Bh8

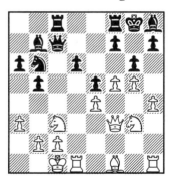

Black had a difficult choice here. In any case his kingside will become very cramped and the scope of his dark squared bishop will be very limited. But moving 17. ... Bd8 is also awkward, for the rooks are blocked from coming to the d8 square to support the backward d-pawn.

Mr. Dillinger is correct — Black's bishop and entire position is awkward after 17. ... Bd8. Still, it was Black's best choice. After 17. ... Bh8 White can win easily by playing 18. f6 and then using old Capablanca's advice: if one piece is cut off, switch the game to the other side of the board, where you'll be playing (and winning) with a de facto *extra piece. Here this technique would have worked perfectly. In the game, White tried to win with a kingside attack, and after some lively play (too lively for the taste of this old pro) succeeded.*

Game 27: Isolani: A Blend of Static Weakness and Dynamic Strength

The positions with an isolated d4 (for Black, d5) pawn, like the one which occurred in the game below on White's tenth move, are the most frequent, and most important, in chess. You should study them well, especially if that pawn structure is likely to occur from openings you play.

Dane Mattson was rated 1791 in September 2005, when he convincingly defeated a 2394-rated opponent. Not surprisingly, Dane is now an expert, and is likely to move much higher.

Writes Dane,

The following is a game that I have intended to submit to *Chess Life* for nearly three years now! Right after I played in this tournament, I lost the scoresheet. Fortunately, I have finally recovered the game. I submit this game today as an expert, but it was a pivotal moment in my chess journey as a sub-1800 player. Although I was paired against an opponent 600 points higher than myself, I maintained my focus on just the pieces and the squares. I was able to win this game while avoiding the psychological pitfalls of playing a much higher-rated opponent. Ratings are great for speculation; playing the games is great for removing speculation.

Queen's Gambit Declined Orthodox Defense [D60]
White: Dane Mattson (1791)
Black: Garush Manukyan (2394)
SuperNationals III, 2005

1. d4 Nf6 2. c4 e6 3. Nc3 d5

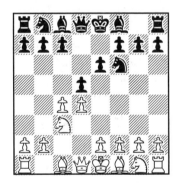

The position is more often reached by a different move order: 1. d4 d5 2. c4 e6 3. Nc3 Nf6.

I remember being surprised at the time that my opponent didn't enter the Nimzo-Indian with 3. ... Bb4. Oftentimes, Black "threatens" the Nimzo, and when White plays 3. Nf3, Black plays 3. ... c5, entering the Modern Benoni while avoiding the sharp Taimanov Variation since White can no longer play f4 before Black castles to safety.

(The Taimanov Variation here is: 1. d4 Nf6 2. c4 c5 3. d5 e6 4. Nc3 exd5 5. cxd5 d6 6. e4 g6 7. f4 Bg7 8. Bb5+.)

4. Nf3 Nbd7 5. Bg5 Be7 6. e3 0-0 7. Bd3 dxc4 8. Bxc4 c5 9. 0-0 cxd4 10. exd4

I now have an isolated queen pawn, but the d4-pawn protects the key e5 and c5 squares. All of my pieces are comfortably developed, while Black still needs to worry about the future of his light-squared bishop.

The side with an isolated d-pawn in this (and similar) positions must first look for an attack. His opponent, naturally, has opposite objectives — to neutralize that attack, in particular by exchanging pieces, thus securing a long-lasting advantage.

10. ... Nb6!?

An interesting idea that attempts to liberate his position via the occupation of the d5 square. Another possibility was 10. ... a6 11. a4 Qc7 *(I doubt the black*

queen belongs on the open c-file — L.A.) 12. Qe2 b6, where Black will soon develop his queen bishop and inherit a slightly passive but relatively solid position.

11. Bd3

I'd prefer 11. Bb3, a popular move which controls the d5 square. If needed, this bishop could be brought to the b1-h7 diagonal later — e.g., after an initial Qd3, thus creating mate-on-h7 motifs.

11. ... Nfd5 12. Bxe7

This exchange is fine, as Black's "good" bishop is indeed a strong protector of his king.

12. ... Qxe7 13. Re1

I always tell my students that rooks have "x-ray vision" and love occupying the same file as the opponent's queen, even if there are pieces in the way.

13. ... f5?

A "You're a 1700 and I'm a 2400" type move that intends to frighten me off the board. A few moments after he played this move, I felt frozen. Was he attempting to play g5-h5 and "steam roll" me off the board? I spent a moment to clear my head, and insisted on analyzing the position, not my opponent's rating. Indeed, with objective analysis, 13. ... f5 is anti-positional, and the backward e6-pawn is very awkward for him.

Absolutely true. Black had to play 13.. ... Bd7, with only a slight advantage for White.

14. Qb3

Creating the threat of 15. Nxd5 Nxd5 16. Qxd5!

14. ... Qf6 15. Nxd5 Nxd5 16. Bc4 Rd8 17. Re5

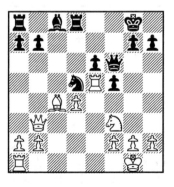

By keeping a clear head, I am punishing my opponent's dubious f-pawn thrust with simple, but potent, improvements of my position that simultaneously worsen his.

17. ... Nc7 18. Rae1

At this point, I am sure Black would love to have the option of playing f5 to f7!

18. ... Re8

This makes White's job easier. But other moves, such as the luft-making 18. ... h6 or "lashing out" with 18. ... b5, are also unlikely to save Black.

19. a4!

I award this move an exclamation mark for my patience in this position. I knew I was in an incredibly good position, and I felt the temptation to rush forward with 19. d5. I felt that after 19. d5 my opponent would have some counterplay with 19. ... b5. I wasn't sure whether or not 19. ... b5 provided sufficient counterplay, but I decided to remove his only counter punch prior to pushing forward with my d-pawn.

If 19. d5 b5 20. Bxb5 Rb8, then 21. d6! wins.

After
21. d6!

But I understand Dane's "pragmatic" choice, 19. a4.

19. ... b5

Desperation. My opponent decided to open his queenside at any cost.

20. axb5 Rb8 21. d5

21. ... Bb7 22. d6
The strongest.
22. ... Nd5 23. d7 Re7

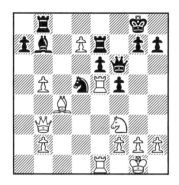

Rather than rushing out a move, I spent the time to calculate the position out to a pleasant conclusion. I calculated that I would loan my queen, but my opponent would have to repay his debt with his king!

24. Bxd5 Bxd5

With a trembling hand, I played . . .

25. Qxd5!

25. Rxd5 also wins, but, of course, 25. Qxd5 is prettier, thus deserving Dane's exclam.

25. ... exd5 26. Rxe7 Qd6 27. Re8+ Kf7

28. Ng5+ Kf6 29. R1e6+ Qxe6 30. Nxe6, Black resigned.

Game 28: What Is My Opponent Planning?

"Prophylaxis: A word used by Nimzowitsch to describe a strategic idea first exemplified by Philidor: the anticipation, prevention, or determent of the opponent's threats."
— *The Oxford Companion to Chess*

Wrote famous coach Mark Dvoretsky, "Under prophylactic thinking, I consider it a good habit to ask yourself, all the time, what one's opponent wants to undertake; how would he move if it were his turn? An ability to find an answer to these questions and take it into account is important during the decision-making process. "

Nathaniel Lagemann used this thinking technique to win. Writes Mr. Lagemann:

I thought perhaps you might be interested in the following annotated game. It took place in my fourth round in the Los Angeles Open. I liked this game because of its positional qualities as well as a nice tactic in the endgame. The tournament ended with me winning 4½/5 and becoming the U1800 champion on tiebreak.

Sicilian Dragon
Yugoslav Attack [B76]
White: Nathaniel Lagemann (1764)
Black: Primo Estillomo (1800)
Los Angeles Open, 2006

1. e4 c5 2. Nf3 d6 3. d4 cxd4 4. Nxd4 g6

5. Be3 Bg7 6. Qd2 Nf6 7. f3 0-0 8. Nc3 Nc6

Although the opening move order was played incorrectly, the game is now entering theoretical lines.

The usual move order is 4. ... Nf6 — to force 5. Nc3. The game line, 4. ... g6, allowed White to get a favorable version of the Maroczy Bind with 5. c4, e.g., 5. ... Nc6 6. Be3. Nathaniel, however, preferred to stay in his familiar Yugoslav Attack.

(In **Chess Openings for Black, Explained**, *Dzindzi, Perelshteyn, and I recommend a following line for Black: 1. e4 c5 2. Nf3 g6 3. d4 cxd4 4. Nxd4 Nc6! 5. c4 Nf6 6. Nc3 Nxd4!, luring the white queen to the d4-square*

which she'll soon have to vacate, losing a tempo.)

9. 0-0-0

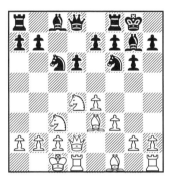

9. ... Re8?!

This move is too passive. A better move would be d5 trying to advance control into the center.

Another good line is 9. ... Bd7.

10. g4

Clearly shows White's plans for a kingside invasion.

10. ... a6 11. h4 Nxd4 12. Bxd4 Be6 13. h5 Qa5

14. Kb1

An immediate 14. Bxf6 Bxf6 15. Nd5 (as happened a move later) does not work, because of

15. ... Qxd2 check.

14. ... b5 15. Bxf6

A slightly better plan would have been 16. h6 Bh8 17. Bxf6 or Nd5. The difference in this variation is the added move h6. This move hems in the Black king.

15. ... Bxf6 16. Nd5 Qxd2 17. Nxf6+

It is a nice in-between move that weakens the "d" pawn.

17. ... exf6 18. Rxd2

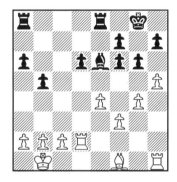

White is stronger here because of Black's isolated pawn on the d-ile and his doubled pawns on the f-file.

18. ... Red8?

Here a better choice for Black would be d5 to trade off the isolated d-pawn for White's stronger e-pawn. A possible continuation is 18. ... d5 19. exd5 Bxd5 20. Bxb5 Bxa2+

After
20. ...
Bxa2+

(20. ... Bxf3 21. Bxe8 Bxh1 22.
Bd7) 21. Kxa2 axb5+ 22. Kb3
Re3+ 23. Rd3 Rxd3+ 24. cxd3
Re8.

19. Be2

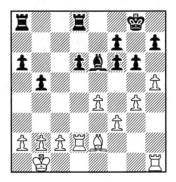

**19. ... Rac8 20. f4 f5 21. exf5
gxf5 22. g5 Kg7 23. h6+ Kf8**

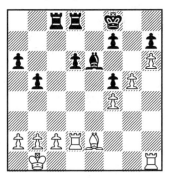

24. Bf3?
Incorrect because it protected

the c4 field from an invasion by
the enemy rook. White's best
move would be Rhd1 doubling
the rooks and adding pressure to
Black's isolated pawn.

*Yes, White would be better —
but Black can hold.*

24. ... Rc4 25. Rh4 d5

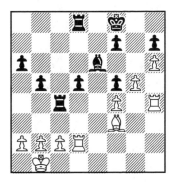

This natural-looking move
weakens Black's dark squared e5
and c5. Black will need to watch
them in the future.

26. b3

This move forces the rook off
of the fourth rank and creates *luft*
(space) for the White king.

26. ... Rc3 27. Bg2

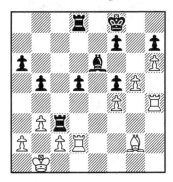

27. ... a5

Black should improve his rook with 27. ... Rg3!

28. Rh3

Offers to trade rooks. Because of White's stronger pawn structures, he is happy to simplify by any piece exchanges.

28. ... b4 29. Rxc3 bxc3 30. Rd4!

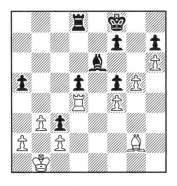

A necessary blocking move. Now, White's rook is preventing the c- and d-pawns from making a chain.

30. ... Ke7 31. Kc1 Rb8 32. a3!

Stops the rook from invading the b4 square.

An excellent case of preventing an opponent's good plan from being implemented.

32. ... Kd6

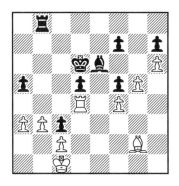

If White succeeds in bringing his king to d4, he'll win easily. Thus Black must look for a counterplay: 32. ... f6!, with some counter-chances.

33. Rd3

At this time it would be a mistake to play 33. Kd1 because of the possible 33. ... Kc5 35. Rd3 d4 which leaves Black with a strong pawn chain.

Another example of prophylactic play.

33. ... Rc8 34. Kd1

White's idea is to eventually bring the king to d4.

Now this plan is unstoppable and winning.

34. ... Rc5 35. Ke2 Kc6 36. a4

36. ... Kd6 37. Ke3
Now the c-pawn is lost.
37. ... Bd7 38. Kd4 Be6 39. Rxc3 Rxc3 40. Kxc3 Kc5 41. Bf3 Bc8 42. Bh5!

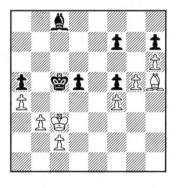

42. ... Be6 43. g6 *(! — L.A.)*
43. ... fxg6 44. Bxg6!

Black cannot recapture the bishop because it will allow the "h" pawn to promote.

White wins one more pawn, and a game.

44. ... Bg8 45. Bxf5, Black resigned.

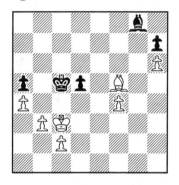

Remember, it is not good enough to just play good moves. You must anticipate and, if possible, block your opponent's good moves too.

Game 29: A C-Player's Ideas On Positional Play

Yes, tactics are the soul of chess; still, we learn and use some basic strategies from our very first steps. Put pawns on e4 and d4; rooks love open files — that sort of thing.

Writes our contributor, Anthony Daniel:

This game is the best reflection of my flawed understanding of positional play. While this example was successful for me, I made terrible mistakes in the realization of my advantage. I was pleased to put my finger on his weakness (d5) which I think shows my growth as a positional player. Right now, I'm beginning to focus more on tactics. This is one of my annotations, and I wouldn't be surprised if you poked some big holes in it. Without further ado here it is.

Irregular Queen's Pawn Opening [A48]
White: Anthony Daniel
Black: Venkat Kausik
Marshall U1600, 2001

1. d4 Nf6 2. Nf3 g6 3. c3

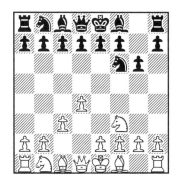

One might argue that White is fixing the pawns a bit early. I argue that against the kingside fianchetto this structure can be tricky to find counterplay against.
3. ... d6 4. Bg5 Bg7 5. Nbd2

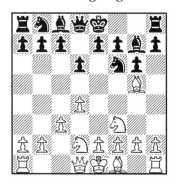

Just so. White sets his eyes on e4. After the e4 thrust, White has leverage in the center.
5. ... Nbd7
It was better first to ask the

white bishop where he wants to go by playing 5. ... h6!. After the likely 6. Bh4 Black enhanced his options (being able to play ... g5 at will), while limiting White's options (no more Be3 retreat).

6. e4

6. ... e5
Of course, Black challenges the white center before it assumes monolithic solidity. 6. ... c5 was also playable, For example, 6. ... c5 7. e5! Ng4? 8. exd6!. However: 6. ... c5 7. e5 dxe5! 8. dxe5 Ng4 9. e6! fxe6 10. Nc4

After
10. Nc4

with compensation for the material. Perhaps my opponent saw this and decided on the more solid ... e5.
7. h3!?

This is to insure the white QB [dark-square bishop] can be kept. This also takes control of g4. This structure has similarities to a Spanish Game and h3 tends to be a useful move in that opening.
7. ... 0-0 8. Bd3!

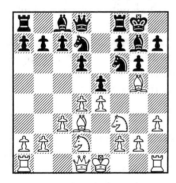

I had quite an argument with myself on whether c4 or d3 was a better square for the bishop. It looks more aggressive on c4, but it can leave the e-pawn loose and it can be exposed to attack. On d3, it is more defensive, but it helps solidify White's space advantage. It could move to c4 if necessary.

This is a correct decision. Another reason in favor of 8. Bd3 — keeping the c4 square free for the white knight.

8. ... b6?!

The double fianchetto isn't exactly wrong but I feel that it doesn't contest the center well enough. Maybe Black should stick to the standard KID sources of counterplay. After all, he did choose a KID setup. Perhaps 8. ... c6 with the idea of Qa5 is better.

Yes, 8. ... c6 and (likely) ... Qc7. And, in general, double fianchetto rarely works well, especially for the second player (Black).

9. 0-0 Bb7 10. Re1 Re8!

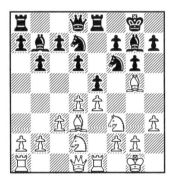

Correct! The e-pawn must be put under pressure. Unfortunately, the pawn cannot be stormed at this point.

11. Qc2

After 11. d5! we'll get a King's Indian-like position where Black's b7-bishop will be restricted by White's pawn — a consequence of 8. ... b6. White

would have been better.

11. ... c5?

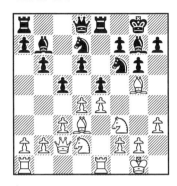

No! This move must be prepared. This move gives White the better game. In order was 11. ... Rc8.

12. Nc4!

With this little knight-hop, White has a considerable advantage. If it was +/= before it must be +/– now. If it isn't +/– it is quite close.

Also good is 12. d5!, with a space advantage — and overall long-lasting advantage for White, who is able to prepare attacks on both sides.

12. ... Qc7 13. dxe5

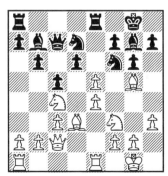

White is moving to ossify the weakness on d5.

13. ... Nxe5 14. Nfxe5!

Only so! The sterling steed on c4 must be maintained to keep advantage.

14. ... dxe5 15. a4!

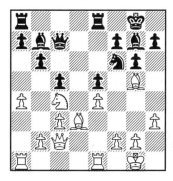

The point of it all. Now White can prepare the invasion Nc4-e3-d5 virtually at his leisure.

15. ... Rad8!

I think this is the best way to fight back. Black must grab the only open file. White is in no position to contest the file — yet.

16. g3!?

I felt White had to reorganize his forces. However 16. Bxf6 Bxf6 17. Ne3 with the idea of Bc4 is better for the white pieces.

Not so easy: 17. ... Bg5!,

After 17. ... Bg5!

ready to exchange the knight.

16. ... Rd7

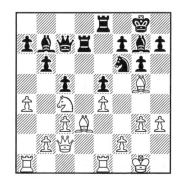

17. Bf1 Red8

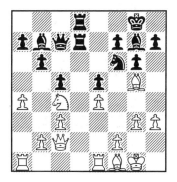

Both sides follow their respective plans.

18. Bg2?

This almost throws the game away. Better is 18. Bxf6 Bxf6 19. Ne3 then 20. Bg2 with advantage for White.

Again, Black meets 19. Ne3 with 19. ... Bg5. (or 19. ... Rd2). Perhaps White should play 18. h4 — after all, the f6-knight is pinned and can't run away.

18. ... Ba6!

Black jumps on his chance to

fight back.
19. Bxf6
White comes back with the move that has been necessary for some time.
19. ... Bxf6

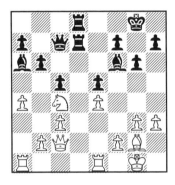

20. Bf1?!
Better was 20. Ne3 but Black now has measurable counterplay.
The more ambitious 20. Ne3 is also somewhat risky for White, e.g., 20. ... Rd2!?.
20. ... Bxc4
Of course.
21. Bxc4 Rd2 22. Qb3

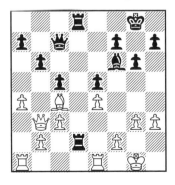

22. ... Bg7?!
I don't think this move is nec-

essary. Maybe 22. ... Kf8 was better.

We've got a position with bishops of opposite color, where queens and four rooks are also on the board and where White's bishop is much more active than Black's. Still, Black's weakness on f7 is easily defendable and his rooks are active. With an accurate defense, Black should draw. Even more attractive is the active 22. ... Qd7, ready to meet 23. h4 (or 23. Kg2 h5 24. h4) with ... Bxh4.
23. Bd5?!

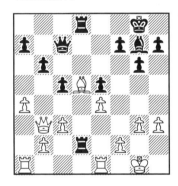

Trading error for error. Better is Rad1 with small advantage for White.
23. ... Rc8!
Black threatens ... c4.
A sacrifice, 23. ... c4, also deserves attention.
24. Rad1?!

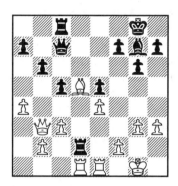

Nope. Better is Bc4. Then we can work on Rad1.

24. ... Rxd1

Better is 24. ... c4! (even stronger now than on the next move, as 25. Qb5 can be met with 25. ... a6).

25. Rxd1 h5?

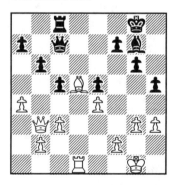

Loses. 25. ... c4 was called for. Slightly better for White is 26. Qb5 a5 but Black has strong drawing chances. With the time limit as it was, 25. ... c4 is almost a guaranteed draw. With more time, of course, Black's defense can get more difficult.

I like 25. ... c4 even now. But

after 25. ... h5 Black is worse but not lost.

26. c4!?

More accurate might be 26. Bc4.

Yes. After 26. Bc4 Bf6 (to prepare ... Rd8) 27. Rd3 Rd8 28. Rf3

After 28. Rf3

Black is passive and must defend carefully.

26. ... Rd8?!

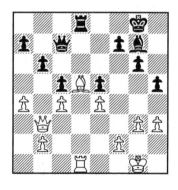

Useless.

Black's best defense is to play 26. Bh6 (or 26. ... Bf8) then ... Kg7 and, if necessary, ... f6.

27. Qb5?!

A much better choice would be 27. a5.

27. ... Qc8?

Wasting time once more.

The move 27. ... a5 puts up more of a fight although White is winning after 28. Rd3!.

After
28. Rd3!

I think winning is too strong a word here.

28. a5!

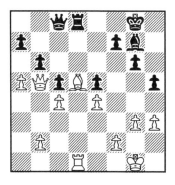

28. ... bxa5 29. Qxa5

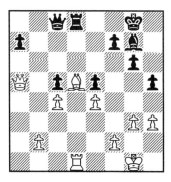

29. ... Rf8
This is tantamount to resignation. Maybe ... Rxd5.
The move 29. ... Rxd5 is in-

deed a resignation, while the passive 29. ... Rf8 loses a pawn, and a game, too. Black's only chance to hold was the simple 29. ... Rd7.

30. Kg2 (rather forced) **Qb8 31. Qa3!**
I would prefer to win the pawn with 31. Qxc5 Qxb2 32. Qxa7.

31. ... Qb6 32. Rd3!

White finds the best win in time pressure. I think 32. Ra1 wins also.

32. ... Qc7
32. ... Rb8 33. Rf3! Qxb2 34. Qxa7

33. Rb3 Rb8 34. Rxb8+ Qxb8 35. Qxc5 Qxb2 36. Qxa7, Black resigns.

The pawns are dropping like ripe fruit.
Anthony's annotations are very good and usually to the point. He knew what to aim for and, aided by his opponent's passive play, deservingly won a tough-fought game.

Part VII
Kids Play and Annotate

Game 30: Outwitting the Professor

Nine-year-old Bethel McGrew was rated (as of June 2002) 996. The quality of her annotations, however, suggests that her rating is likely to double in the near future.

Writes Bethel:

I am enclosing a game that I played this April in the hope that you will be able to use it for your "Back to Basics" column in *Chess Life*. It is one of the best games I have played so far.

I am nine years old and home-schooled. I have played in three tournaments, and my USCF rating is 996. I go to two chess clubs a week and study chess with my dad, who is my coach.

This game was played at my house against a math professor from Chicago who was visiting us. In the opening I offer a gambit which he unwisely accepts, allowing me to get a grip on the center. Although Black does not make any obvious blunders, he does miss some tactics.

Vienna Game [C29]
White: Bethel McGrew (996)
Black: Eric Vestrup
casual game, 2002

1. e4 e5 2. Nc3 Nf6 3. f4

3. ... exf4?

This is a mistake, since it allows Black's knight to be kicked around. The best move here is 3. ... d5.

4. e5

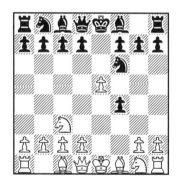

4. ... Ng8 5. Nf3

Stopping an obnoxious queen check at h4.

5. ... g6?

This is a passive move. Black should try to neutralize my advantage in space with 5. ... d6.

After
5. ... d6

6. d4

White seizes the chance to make a solid center.

6. ... Bb4

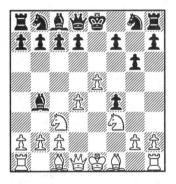

To play 6. ... Bb4 (after first playing 5. ... g6) is illogical — and bad.

7. a3?

This move is not necessary. I should continue developing my pieces with 7. Bxf4 and ignore the pin on the knight.

Very good point. It also illustrates that we should learn to find our own errors even in games we won.

7. ... Bxc3+ 8. bxc3 f6 9. Bxf4

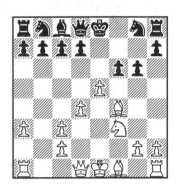

This is a good developing move that regains my material and defends the pawn.

9. ... fxe5 10. Bxe5

Also very strong is 10. dxe5!, hindering Black's development.

10. ... Nf6 11. Bc4

If Black tries to kick my bishop back with 11. ... d5, I can remove the guard and win the d-pawn with 12. Bxf6 and 13. Bxd5. If he doesn't kick the bishop, he has trouble castling.

*In fact, 12. Bxf6 (after 11. .. d5) removes **two** defenders!*

11. ... d6

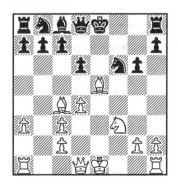

12. Bf4?!

This is not a bad move, but I could simply take the knight on f6: 12. Bxf6 Qxf6 13. 0-0

After
13. 0-0

and Black should be uneasy about his exposed king and the (possible) discovered attack on his queen.

100% correct.

12. ... Qe7+ 13. Qe2 Qxe2+ 14. Kxe2 Ne4?!

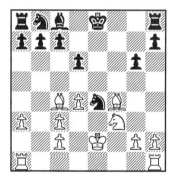

This is a risky move, since White can threaten to pin the knight.

It's also risky because Black moves his only developed piece for the second time.

15. Rhe1!

Threatening a discovered check if black takes the pawn. I am also setting up a pin on the black knight.

A truly great move.

15. ... Bf5 16. Kf1

The trap is sprung.

16. ... Kd7

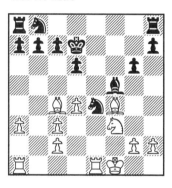

17. Bd5!

A very good move that wins material. Notice that I put another attacker on the knight and at the same time threaten to win the exchange.

17. ... Nc6?

This move gives up more than Black has to. It would be better to give up the exchange with 17. ... Nxc3 18. Bxb7 Nc6 19. Bxa8 Rxa8.

After
19. ...
Rxa8

White is still winning, but it would be more difficult for me.

Now the game is over.

18. Bxe4

18. ...Bxe4 19. Rxe4 d5 20. Re2

Moving my rook just far enough back that my other rook can come to the e-file.

Very good.

20. ... Rhf8 21. Bh6 Rf5 22. Kg1

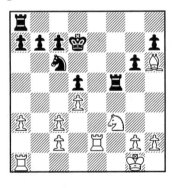

Unpinning my knight.

22. ... Re8?

This is not a good move. Since I am a piece ahead, it is not a good idea for Black to trade pieces.

23. Rxe8 Kxe8 24. Re1+ Ne7 25. Bg5!

One of my dad's favorite sayings is that you should torment a pinned piece. This is no exception.

25. ... Rf7 26. Ne5, Black resigns.

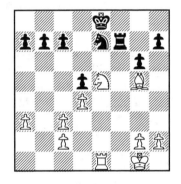

I suppose I was a little sorry that he resigned here, since I was hoping for the following tactics: 26. ... Rf8?? (26. ... Rg7 27. Bf6 Rg8 28. Nf3, winning the knight on e7), 27. Bxe7! Kxe7 28. Nxg6++ and 29. Nxf8.

Games 31 & 32: Two Upsets

Eve Zhurbinski won two big upset games in the Amateur Team East of 2005. Both games are exciting, well-played by Eve (even if not flawless) and very thoroughly annotated by her.

Writes Eve:

Enclosed you will find my games against two opponents rated about 500 points higher than me from the U.S. Amateur Team East tournament in Parsippany, NJ.

I'm eight years old and it was my first participation in a team tournament. I played second board for the Westfield Future Stars team. Each game was the second biggest upset in its round (1 and 3).

Queen's Gambit Declined
[D35]
White: Thomas Frederick (1687)
Black: Eve Zhurbinski (1229)
Amateur Team East 2005

1. d4 d5 2. c4 e6 3. Nc3 Nf6 4. cxd5 exd5 5. Bg5 Bb4

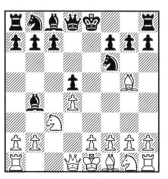

6. a3 Bxc3+ 7. bxc3 0-0 8. Nf3 Nbd7 9. e3 c6 10. Bd3

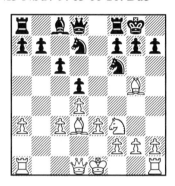

10. ... Re8
Better was 10. ... h6 because White had to decide where to put the bishop.

11. 0-0 Qc7?!
Again, I needed to go 11. ... h6 first, to know where the black square bishop will be located, before advancing my queen. Now White has a big advantage.

I would prefer 11 ... Qa5 (see Black's 13th move) and then ... Ne4 — similar to the game but with an extra tempo.

12. Qc2 Ne4 13. Bf4 Qa5 14. c4 Ndf6

15. cxd5

It was better to go 15. c5, to put pressure on the b7-pawn.

15. ... cxd5 16. Bc7?

Bad move! White lost time because the attack of the queen is not dangerous. The bishop is in a bad position on c7, and it was better to play Rfc1, putting pressure on the square, than to occupy it. Now Black can finish developing his pieces.

16. ... b6 17. Rfc1 Ba6 18. Bxa6 Qxa6 19. Qb2 Rac8 20. Bf4

20. ... Nh5?!

Analyzing this position after the game, I discovered that 20. ... Ng4 21. Rf1 Rc3 was more dangerous.

21. Be5 Rxc1+ 22. Rxc1 Rc8 23. h3 h6 24. g4?!

Not the best move because it weakens the king's position.

24. ... Nhf6

25. Bh2??

Blunder! White should exchange rooks first.

The crucial moment of the game. 25. Rxc8+, suggested by Eve, followed by 26. Bxf6 allows White to hold, while 25. Bh2 loses a pawn and a game.

25. ... Rxc1+ 26. Qxc1 Qe2

27. Qc8+

The move 27. Ne5 does not help White as well because 27. ... Qxf2+ 28. Kh1 Nh7!

After 28. ... Nh7!

with the idea of Nf8.

Very nice defense!

27. ... Kh7 28. Qf5+ g6 29. Qf4 Qxf2+ 30. Kh1

30. ... Qf1+ 31. Bg1 Nf2+, White resigns.

There will be a mate on the next move.

Petroff's Defense [C42]
White: Christopher Sugino (1702)
Black: Eve Zhurbinski (1229)
Amateur Team East 2005

1. e4 e5 2. Nf3 Nf6 3. Nc3 Bb4

4. d3

This passive move gives Black a pawn on KP4 (e5) vs. White's pawn on QP3 (d3), and a small edge (compare with positions reached after 1. e4 e5 2. Nf3 Nc6 3. Bb5 d6 4. d4 exd4 5. Nxd4).

After 5. Nxd4

Better 4. Nxe5 or 4. Bc4, with equality.

4. ... d5

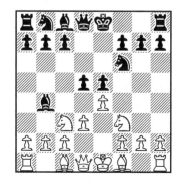

5. exd5 Nxd5 6. Bd2 Nc6 7. Be2 0-0 8. 0-0 Re8 9. a3

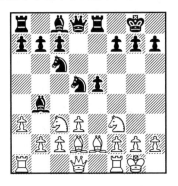

9. ... Nxc3

In a very similar position with reversed colors (the only difference being that the rook pawn was on second rank rather than the third) Tarrasch played B-KB1 (Bf1). That game, Tarrasch-Vogel 1910, is one of the all-time classics.

10. bxc3

Stronger was 10. Bxc3! White is cramped and should welcome trades.

10. ... Bc5 11. Be3?!

Not the best move. Now Black could simply take the

bishop and destroy White's pawn structure: 11. ... Bxe3 12. fxe3 e4.

After 12. ... e4

But I made a bad move as well.
11. ... Bd6? 12. Nd2 f5!

13. f3?

That's bad. Now the white square bishop has no moves. It was better to play 13. Nc4 or Nb3.
13. ... b6 14. Nc4

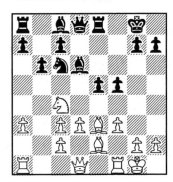

14. ... Be7?!

It was better to play 14. ... f4, ... Qg5, and ... Bh3 to attack the king flank.

15. f4 Bf6 16. fxe5 Nxe5 17. Nxe5 Bxe5

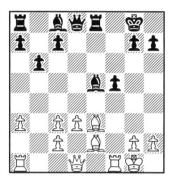

18. Bd2??

This is a blunder! White lost the fight for the black squares. He should play 18. Qd2.

True. 18. Qd2 allows Black to win a pawn, but after 18. ... Bxc3 19. Qxc3 Rxe3 20. Bf3 Rb8 21. Rae1

After 21. Rae1

White's activity provides good compensation.

After 18. Bd2 Black has a strong attack: 18. ... Qh4 19. h3

(Another line which I'd guess Eve saw is 19. g3 Bxg3! 20. hxg3 Qxg3+ 21. Kh1

After 21. Kh1

21. ... Rxe2! and 22. ... Bb7+, winning.)
19. ... Qg3 20. Rf3 Qh2+ 21. Kf2 Bb7, but I made not the best move:

18. ... Qd6?!

putting the queen behind the bishop.

19. h3 Bxc3 20. Bxc3 Qc5+

21. d4 Qxc3 22. Bf3 Rb8 23.

Bd5+ Kh8 24. Rf3 Re3

25. Kf2?! (Rxe3) **Rxf3+ 26. Bxf3 Ba6! 27. Rb1 Rd8 28. d5**

28. ... Qxa3

Simpler was 28. ... c6 with the idea of ... Qc5+.

Yes. And if you're much better (or winning) — try not to give your opponent any meaningful counterplay.

29. Qd4 Qc5

Black has an easy win after 29. ... Qa2 30. Ra1 Qxc2+ 31. Kg1 Qd3 but I made a terrible mistake by trying to simplify the position. Now Black has lost all advantage.

30. Qxc5 bxc5 31. Ra1 Rd6 32. Ra5 c4 33. Rc5 Rd7

34. Be2?

Because of my low rating, White tried to play for the win. But it would be better for them to force a draw by repetition of moves: 34. Ra5 Rd6 35. Rc5 Rd7 36. Ra5 Rd6 37. Rc5 Rd7 38. Ra5. After 34. Be2 Black has a better position.

34. ... g5

Better 34. ... g6, keeping the kingside pawns well protected.

35. Kf3

Stronger was 35. Ra5 or — if White wanted to move the king — 35. Ke3.

35. ... Kg7 36. Bxc4?!

Again, 36. Ra5 was a better decision.

36. ... Bxc4 37. Rxc4 Kf6

38. Ra4?

More persistent was Rc5.

The line 38. Rc5 Ke5 39. d6+ shows why the prudent 34. ... g6 was stronger than 34. ... g5.

38. ... Rxd5 39. Rxa7 Rc5 40. Ra6+

40. ... Ke5

I'd prefer 40. ... c6 (see my next comment.)

41. Rh6

It was better for White to defend the c-pawn with 41. Ra2.

No. Being a pawn down, with a passive rook and restricted (after 41. ... Rc3) king is hopeless for White, who will have to watch

helplessly how Black steadily improves the position of her king and her kingside pawns.

41. ... Rxc2

Black should first check with the rook on c3 to take the pawn with a tempo. But even the move from the game is enough for a win.

42. Rxh7

42. ... Rc3+ 43. Ke2

Better 43. Kf2, with the following division of labor: white king protects his pawns, leaving the rook active. At the very least, this would make Black's road to victory more difficult!

43. ... c5 44. Re7+ Kf4 45. Kd2 Rg3

46. Re2 c4 47. Kc2 c3 48. Rf2+ Ke5 49. Re2+ Kd4 50. Rf2 f4

51. h4?
White's last mistake.
51. ... Ke3 52. Rf3+ Rxf3 53. gxf3 gxh4, White resigns.

Game 33: Analyzing Together

"Post-Mortem: Examination of a game soon after it has ended.
Players often crowd the board throwing in their comments.
... sometimes used as a basis for published annotation ..."
— *The Oxford Companion to Chess.*

Unless a new round starts shortly, it's always good to go over just-finished games with your opponent. Spectators (and readers) also benefit from listening to both opponents' recollections and opinions. I remember enjoying the mandatory joint press conferences/ post-mortems after each game of the Kasparov-Anand match in New York City. And one of the best books ever written on world championships compiled notes of GMs Isaac Boleslavsky and Igor Bondarevsky, coaches, respectively, of World Champion Tigran Petrosian and challenger Boris Spassky.

Thus, I welcomed the joint analyses of Igor Ummel and Robert Karch.

Writes Robert Karch:

The game Ummel-Karch spans the generations! Igor is ten years old: I am 75. We both have included notes to the game.

Igor Ummel's notes will be in regular type, and Robert Karch's in *italics* [and my comments will be in brackets].

Bird's Opening [A02]
White: Igor Ummel (1660)
Black: Robert Karch (1742)
2005 Washington Class

1. f4
I always like to play the Bird Opening because the positions that arise from it are unique.
1. ... Nf6 2. Nf3 d6

3. b3?!
I usually play 3. e3 here. I was afraid of ... Bg4. The problem is that now Black can play ... c5, which you want to prevent.
[I'd prefer, yes, 3. e3. I don't think 3. ... Bg4 is so good for Black; besides, if Black wants, he can play 3. . .. Bg4 after 3. b3 as well.]
As Black, I didn't have a specific plan other than to survive into the middlegame.
3. ... c5

He plays 3. ... c5 as I feared.

Black misses the fork idea 3.
... e5 4. fxe5 dxe5 5. Nxe5? Qd4,
winning a piece. White would
sidestep this, of course, but Black
would benefit by opening lines
for his two bishops.

4. Bb2 Nc6 5. e3

5. ... a6

A bit slow, but I wanted to
keep the White bishop off the
dangerous c4-f7 diagonal.

[Black's 5. ... a6 also stops 6.
Bb5 — read Igor's comment to
his sixth move.]

6. Be2

Here my bishop is in the way.
Usually in the Bird you want to
get rid of the light-squared
bishop by Bb5, but here Black's
pawn on a6 protects b5.

6. ... g6

[Black allows 7. Bxf6, as the
emerging position — worth your
study — favors him.]

7. 0-0 Bg7 8. h3

Preparing a possible g2-g4
push and protecting the g4
square.

8. ... 0-0 9. Qe1?

How can I miss Black's next
move?

9. ... Nb4

**10. Bd1 b5 11. d3 Bb7 12.
Nbd2 Nbd5**

I see a potential double
attack, which is largely oppor-
tunistic, exploiting the unpro-
tected white bishop on b2.

13. a3?

I missed a simple fork. Best is
13. c4.

[If 13. c4, then 13. ... Nb4 14.
Qe2 Nh5 15. Bxg7 Ng3!. Perhaps 13. d4 is White's best defense here.]

13. ... Nxe3 14. Qxe3 Nd5 15. Qe4 Bxb2 16. Rb1

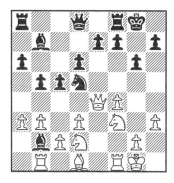

16. ... Bc3!

Essential to the combination, preventing the advance of the c-pawn and then White would win the pinned knight.

If 16. ... Bg7 17. c4 wins a piece.

[More precisely, it wins two minor pieces for a rook — and Black then can draw after 17. ... Nc3 18. Qxb7 Rb8 by harassing the white queen. But why should Black allow a draw, being pawn up? Thus, 16. ... Bc3 deserves Robert's exclam.]

17. g3

Here I realized that my opponent is a tactical player. So I decided to play positionally (my favorite type of style) to make him have a hard time.

17. ... Rb8

[Better was 17. ... Qd7, protecting the b7-bishop while attacking White's h3-pawn.]

18. Qe1

A discovery was threatened.

18. ... Qc7 [18. ... Qa5!] **19. Qf2**

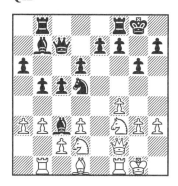

19. ... Ba5

[Black prepares to relocate his bishop onto the wrong diagonal (a7-g1.) The "normal" 19. ... Bg7 was much stronger by comparison. And why not the straightforward 19. ... Qa5!, going for a second pawn?]

20. Ne4 Bb6?

Yes, Black threatens 21. ... c4 but my c4 stops his threat and improves my position.

In general, I think that it is a good idea to aim your pieces at the opposing king. There is also a potential skewer against the White queen.

[In this disagreement, as you already know, I firmly side with Igor.]

21. c4 Nf6

The only place to go.

The exchange of knights on f6 will saddle Black with doubled pawns, and at least partially compensate White for his one-pawn deficit.

[Yet another — very concrete — reason to put a question mark to 20. ... Bb6. Earlier, Black was almost winning, now, he is simply better.]

22. Nxf6+ exf6

Now Black's extra pawn is worthless.

All too true!

23. Nd2

Planning 24. Bf3.

23. ... Rbd8 24. Bf3

[Black had to play 23. ... d5, as now 24. Ne4 holds. But White, fixed on his plan (typical for us all, isn't it?) missed the opportunity.]

24. ... d5

Best.

25. Qg2

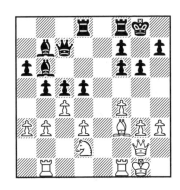

25. ... f5 26. Rfe1 Rd7 27. Re5 Rfd8 28. Kh2?

Bad move.

[Yes, White underestimates Black's d-file pin. Stronger was 28. Nf1.]

28. ... dxc4 29. Bxb7

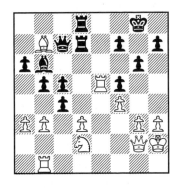

29. ... Rxd3??

Black had a huge advantage after 29. ... Qxb7, according to Fritz. After he played 29. ... Rxd3?? it went from a huge advantage for Black to equal or slightly better for White!

And yet, at the board, with neither of us having access to a computer, I was feeling opti-

mistic!

[I agree with Robert that the position after 29. … Rxd3 *may* be better, perhaps even much better for Black — amid many complications. But why seek complication when a simple move (29. … Qxb7) leaves Black two pawns up? Don't muddy up an already-won game!]

30. Nf1 cxb3

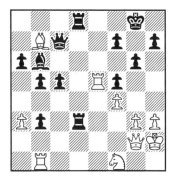

I give Black's move a question mark. It does look like a good move, but if White plays correctly, the pawns should be stopped.

I felt that the two connected passed pawns would be worth more than the White bishop.

[I think both comments apply more to the decision to sacrifice the bishop — 29. … Rxd3 — than to Black's choice of a 30th move. My choice would be 30. ... Rxb3, as after 31. Rxb3 cxb3 White, with only one rook left, would not be able to stop Black's pawn avalanche.]

31. Bxa6

The only move!

31. … c4 32. Bxb5

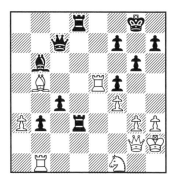

32. ... Rc3 33. Rb2 Bd4

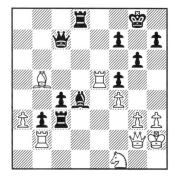

This fork is decisive.

[Here Igor and Robert clearly disagree, — see Igor's comments to his next move — each feeling his side is winning (Igor) or at least better (Robert). Personally, I'd prefer Black.]

34. Ree2??

A big blunder. 34. Re1 should have won! Now the b2-rook doesn't have a flight to e2.

[34. Re1 (indeed the best) 34. ... Rd3 35. Rbe2 b2 hardly "wins" for White.]

34. ... Rc1 35. Rbd2 c3

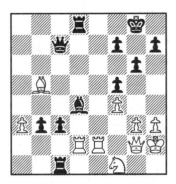

The passed pawns begin to pay off.

36. Bd3

[Equals resignation. White, with nothing to lose, should have tried a wild counter-attack: 36. Rxd4 Rxd4 37. Re8+ Kg7 38. Qa8. Black still would have to work to win!]

36. ... cxd2 37. Nxd2 Bg1+ 38. Kh1 Rxd3, White resigns.

Part VIII
The Endgame

Game 34: The King's Power

With only a few pieces left, a well-centralized king
is a big force — use it!

Just a few hours spent on studying endings should greatly improve your results!

Writes William Franklin:

I recently played in the Ohio Senior Championship and although I finished with only 1.5 out of 5 points since I played in the OPEN section up against Master and Expert level players I learned a lot.

I present my best game from that tournament and hopefully an instructive one - I took your advice from the Franklin Tango article about improving my endgame and I think this game does show improvement.

The real highlight of this game occurs in the endgame. Both players offered draws leading up to the final moments and were subsequently rejected as I aggressively tried for the win, only to have brilliant counterplay by Morgan force the draw.

(It would be interesting to know when the draws were offered, as well as the time used by players on each move — or, at least, in crucial moments. — L.A.).

Ruy Lopez
Worrall Variation [C86]
White: William Franklin (1658)
Black: Morgan Everett (2049)
Ohio Sr. Championship 2010
            Toledo, OH.

**1. e4 e5 2. Nf3 Nc6 3. Bb5 a6
4. Ba4 Nf6 5. Qe2 b5**

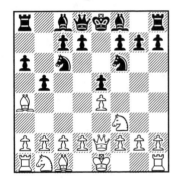

The Worrall variation in the Ruy Lopez is noted by White playing a queen move, Qe2 on Move 5, which constrains a lot of options for Black, such as playing into the Open Ruy Lopez.

6. Bb3 Bc5 7. c3 0-0 8. d3 d6

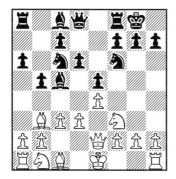

9. Be3 Qe7 10. Nbd2 Bg4

Does Black really want to exchange this bishop for a knight? I don't think so.

11. Nf1 Rab8

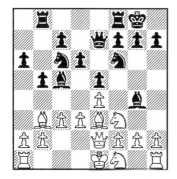

12. Ng3

I'd prefer 12. h3, preventing the exchange that follows. If 12. ... Be6, then 13. Ng3 — knight goes to f5.

12. ... Nh5 13. Nxh5 Bxh5 14. Bxc5 dxc5 15. 0-0 Kh8 16. Qe3 Rbd8

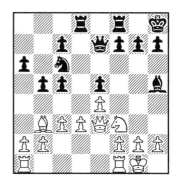

Black is playing aggressively with the bishop at g4 to h5, and attacking White's central pawn structure with the rook move.

And White reacts too defensively, see his next move, 17. Ne1. Instead, 17. Bd5! creates problems for Black; it's Black who has to struggle for equality.

17. Ne1 f5 18. exf5 Rxf5 19. f3

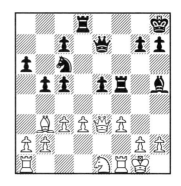

19. ... Bg6 20. Rd1 Qd6 21. Rd2 Rf6 22. Bc2

22. ... h6 23. Rdf2 *(23. Re2! — LA)* **23. ... Ne7**

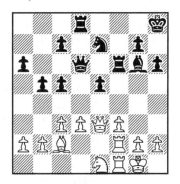

24. f4 exf4 25. Rxf4 Nd5 26. Rxf6 Nxe3 27. Rxd6

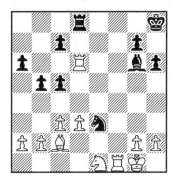

27. ... cxd6?

After another recapture, the simple 27. ... Rxd6, White would be facing more serious problems.
28. Rf2 Nxc2 29. Rxc2 c4 30. Rd2 Re8 31. Kf2 Rf8+ 32. Kg1

32. ... d5 33. dxc4 dxc4 34. Rd6 Rf6

35. Rd2 Be4 36. g3

I decided not to exchange rooks despite the fact it would leave Black with two pawn islands. Instead I felt that I needed the rook at this point to sustain a draw, since Black now has the advantage with the bishop over the knight in an open position with pawns on both the kingside and queenside. White's knight is in a dismal position and needs to be activated, which I proceed to do by moving it to the kingside and then acting as a shield for the white king to advance to the center and possibly the queenside.

Not capturing on f6 on the 35th move was a wrong judgement! After 35. Rxf6 gxf6 36. Kf2 and then 37. Ke3 and 38. Kd4, White is clearly better (analyze this endgame!). Also wrong was 36. g3, expanding the reach of the black bishop.

36. ... Kh7 37. a3 g5 38. Rf2 Kg6 39. Rd2

39. ... g4
This should have led to a quick draw. After 39. ... h5, White has problems to resolve.

40. Ng2 Kg5
A serious error! 40. ... Bxg2 was a must. White's knight on f4 will soon dominate Black's bishop, in coordination with White's other pieces.

41. Nf4 Bf3 42. Kf2 Kf5 43. Rd8 Ke5 44. Ke3 Rf7 45. Rh8

Rf6 46. Re8+

46. ... Kd6
The black king is driven from the center; the white king can now enter.

47. Rd8+
Stronger was the natural 47. Kd4, as well as 47. h4.

47. ... Kc5 48. Rd4 a5 49. Rd8 Rb6 50. Re8 Rd6 51. Re5+ Kb6 52. Re6 Kc5

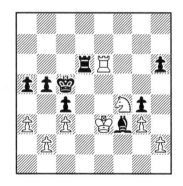

53. Rxd6 Kxd6 54. Kd4 Bc6 55. Ng6 Bb7 56. Ne5 h5

I finally trade off the rooks under favorable conditions for White and Black's bishop is starting to look bad while the white knight becomes more active attacking both sides with possible forks.

And, most importantly, White's king is dominant!

57. Nf7+

Now 57. a4 wins a pawn, with a winning advantage. Black could have prevented this by himself playing a5-a4, for instance on the 54th move — but even there White should have won first some pawn, and then a game, albeit not so easily.

57. ... Ke7 58. Ne5 Ke6 59. Ng6 Kf5 60. Nf4 h4 61. Kc5

This move opens the black king a route to f3, and leads to a draw, while both 61. a4 and 61. Nd5 win easily. (In a pawn ending after 61. Nd5 Bxd5, Black's king would be put into Zugzwang, and the g4 pawn would fall).

61. ... Ke4 62. Kxb5 hxg3 63. hxg3 Kf3 64. Nh5

64. ... Bd5 65. Kxa5 Bf7 66. Nf6 Kxg3 67. Nxg4 Kxg4 68. Kb4 Kf4 69. a4 Ke4 70. a5 Kd3

Draw agreed.

I could have waited another move instead of taking the g4-pawn but the outcome would have been the same.

(But, if you can get some advantage — here a tempo — for free, why not do it? L.A.)

Black's powerful bishop placement along with the anchored c4 pawn negates any White advantage. It was a tedious game and I was excited by the fact I had a possible winning position, only to watch Black come up with brilliant moves to thwart my advantages.

Yes, in the very end Black defended well. And Mr. Franklin's overall achievements: coming from behind, outplaying his Expert opponent in the ending, and drawing from the position of strength, are quite impressive. But there is clearly a lot of room for further improvement, especially in the endgame.

In the earlier game Mr.

Franklin referred to, he used an opening novelty and soon achieved a somewhat better ending against Expert Robert Feldstein (Mr. Franklin's rating was then — in 2009 — just 1437). Later, in the position below, they agreed to a draw.

White, of course, has real winning — and Black has real drawish — chances here. And, both being in time pressure, Mr. Franklin's acceptance of a draw was quite reasonable. However, while his play, and his notes, were of A-player quality, his endgame analyses were quite poor. *E.g.* in this position

After 51. ... Ka6

he wrote: if White plays 52. Kd4, Black counters with 52. ... Kb5. But that position is a win for

White. Here is how you should think: If a straight line (52. Kd4 Kb5 53. Ke5) doesn't work, ask yourself what if, in a diagrammed position, it was Black to move? The answer is, White wins: 1. ... Kb7 2. Kd4 Ka6 (or 2. ... Kc7) 3. Ke5. And how to give Black a move? Easy: 52. Kd4 Kb5 53. Kc3! And now if 53. ... Ka6 54. Kc4 (same position, Black to move) and if 53. ... Ka4 also 54. Kc4, winning.

Game 35:
The Pawn Endgame Roller Coaster

"The [endgame] is as important as the opening and middlegame ... three of the five losses sustained by Bronstein in his drawn match with Botvinnik in 1951 were caused by weak endgame play." — *The Oxford Companion to Chess*

No stage of the game reveals the true powers of the pieces as does the endgame. So said Jose Raoul Capablanca, recommending to start chess studies with that final stage of the game.

The game below demonstrates how practically useful the basic knowledge of endgames is for players of *all* levels. Contributor Paul Berg and his much higher-rated opponent struggled mightily, and quite well, until entering the knight ending, and especially the pawn ending. There, for a while, every move of both players was an obvious (to those who know the basics) blunder, capable of changing a won position into a drawn, or even a lost one — only if an opponent knew how to take advantage of it rather than replying with his own blunder.

Because I've found this ending so instructive, I'll be somewhat brief in commenting on other stages of this game!

Back to Endgame Basics
Writes Mr. Berg:

I recently played a game in a four-week-long tournament (one game each Friday night) at the Boca Raton Chess Club (Florida). I believe there is much to learn from this game, especially since I was playing up in an Under-2000 section and my opponent was 500 rating points higher than me.

I am a member of the Archbishop McCarthy High School Chess Team. Last year, we finished third at Nationals in the Under1200 Division (out of about 70 teams!) We will play in the Under1500 this year.

I really want to know what you have to say!

As you will see, Black holds strong until the last few crucial moves.

Ruy Lopez, Closed [C96]
White: Eric Ramento (1670)
Black: Paul Berg (1173)
Boca Raton CC U2000

**1. e4 e5 2. Nf3 Nc6 3. Bb5 a6
4. Ba4 Nf6 5. 0-0 Be7 6. Re1 b5**

7. Bb3 0-0

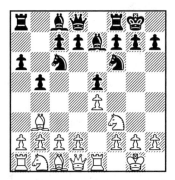

All book as far as I know. It continues with White's idea of c3 and bringing the bishop back.

8. c3 d6 9. h3 Na5 10. Bc2 c5

Here I have always preferred the Black side of this position because of superior development.

No. This is the normal, "classic," theoretical position with chances for both players.

11. d4 cxd4

Black has here many choices, most popular still being the "ancient" 11. ... Qc7.

12. cxd4 Bb7

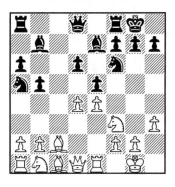

As Paul soon discovers, this doesn't lose a pawn. In fact,

White's best is 13. d5, with chances for a small edge.

13. dxe5 dxe5 14. Qxd8 Rfxd8 15. Nxe5 Rac8

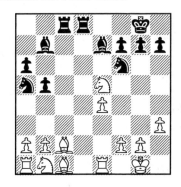

It turns out to be almost like a sacrifice. I did not notice until analysis that winning back the pawn would be easy.

16. Bb3

I was surprised at this because he is going to double up his pawns and then I can win back the pawn I am down.

True. Better was 16. Bd3, and White holds.

16. ... Nxb3 17. axb3 Nxe4 18. Be3

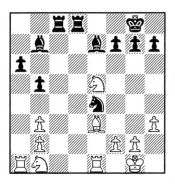

18. ... Bc5

I felt this was a good move. What do you think?

I'd prefer here 18. ... Bb4, to force 19. Rf1 retreat. Still after 18. ... Bc5 Black is clearly better in all lines.

19. Bxc5 Rxc5 20. Ng4 Rc2

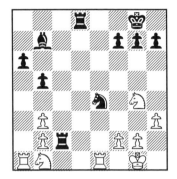

I thought here possibly ... f5 then ... f4 eventually almost forcing a knight retreat to h2 or d1 then I could take on the seventh rank as soon as it was available.

21. f3 Nc5

Good square for the knight.

22. b4 Nb3 23. Ra2 Kf8

I wanted to bring the other rook into play and eliminate back rank mates.

24. Ne3 Rc1 25. Rxc1 Nxc1 26. Ra3 Rd3 27. Kf2 Rd4

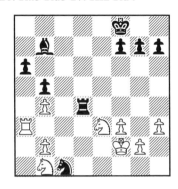

Winning a pawn.

28. Rc3 Nd3+ 29. Ke2 Nxb4 30. Rc7

Cleverly trying to win my rook if the bishop is misplaced.

For a lost pawn White got some initiative, but this initiative is temporary, and Paul skillfully neutralized it in a few next moves. Note Black's important, and untouchable, knight.

30. ... Bc6 31. Rc8+ Be8 32. Nc3

32. ... g6 *(! — L.A.)* **33. Rc7 Rd7 34. Rc8 Ke7 35. Ne4 a5**

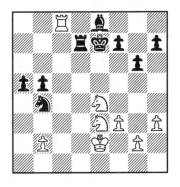

36. Ng4 f5

I now have only 11 minutes left on my clock.

37. Rxe8+ Kxe8 38. Ngf6+ Ke7 39. Nxd7

39. ... Kxd7

Here I should have taken the other knight, not losing my h-pawn, but I guess that is what time pressure does to you.

Paul did well to find this in-between-move — even if after the game. After 39. ... fxe4, Black is up a pawn — and winning.

40. Nf6+ Ke7 41. Nxh7 Nc6

42. Ng5 a4 43. Kd2 Kd6 44. f4 Kc5 45. Nf3 Nd4

Here I thought White could play 46. Ne5.

This threat to win a pawn will force Black to counter-attack — and Black clearly has all the fun! After 46. Ne5 Kb4 Black will checkmate or obtain a new queen.

46. Ne1 b4 47. Nd3+ Kc4 48. Nc1

48. ... Nb3+

Of course! This pawn ending is easily won for Black.

49. Kc2 Nxc1 50. Kxc1

Now I have the winning move, 50. ... Kd3. I also have only two minutes on my clock, and I thought I could queen either the a- or b-pawn!

Not with his king able to reach the b1-square.

50. ... Kb3 51. Kb1

51. ... a3

It's still not too late to win: 51. ... Kc4 52. g4 Kd5, and if 53. g5, then Ke4 — just in time!

52. bxa3

With only two minutes left, it's easy to err. Still, with the white king on b1, neither a-, or b-pawn can possibly queen. Thus, Black had to capture with a pawn and then run to the kingside.

52. ... Kxa3

53. Ka1
*Now White missed a win: 53.
g4 creating a far-off passed pawn
which the black king now can't
stop.*
**53. ... b3 54. Kb1 b2 55. g4
fxg4 56. hxg4**

56. ... Kb3
*Black loses, holding for too
long to his (now worthless) b-
pawn. 56. ... Kb4 was a must, as
the black king is in the square of
the f-pawn, and as in the case of
57. f5 gxf5 58. g5 both sides will
queen. Still, 57. g5 Kc5 58. f5
Kd6 59. f6 wins for White.*
57. f5
Now it's all over.
57. ... gxf5 58. gxf5 Ka3
What Black is hoping for?
**59. f6 Kb3 60. f7 Kc3 61.
f8=Q, Black resigned.**
A painful loss but a learning
experience.
*I don't know how much time
White had — but even with very
little time both sides should have
seen that White, after securing
the b1-square, must play g4, and
that Black must race to the kingside.*
*I hope that a gift I've chosen
for Paul — a copy of* **Just the
Facts (Endgame Knowledge in
One Volume)** *by Nikolai Krogius
— will help Paul to win won endings (and some drawn or even
lost endings) in the future.*

Game 36: Draw on Demand, or When To Reset Your Goals Much Higher

To force a draw on an unwilling opponent, especially an equal (or stronger) opponent, isn't an easy task. Not even for World Champions. Not even with white pieces.

In my opinion, the best way to play against a stronger opponent is to remain true to yourself. Just keep looking for best moves! Only if given an opportunity to enforce a draw (say, by a perpetual check), take your opponent's rating into account.

Our contributor, Dr. Douglas Lee Strout, adopted a more direct "gimme-a-draw" strategy and succeeded in it. In fact, in the end of the game, he could — and should, I think —play for a win.

**Alekhine Defense
(by transposition) [B02]**
White: Dr. Douglas Lee Strout
(1107)
Black: Christian B. Chavez
(1764)
Chess Place Atlanta June Open
2007
1. e4

This is without a doubt my best game ever. As is usual for a Swiss open section, I get a first-round opponent who is way over my head rating-wise. Christian Chavez will draw with me, win all his remaining games, and finish with 3½/4 for clear second in the tournament.
1. ... d5 2. exd5 Nf6

**3. Nc3 Nxd5 4. Nxd5 Qxd5
5. Qf3**

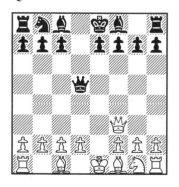

The hunt is on.

Of course, White often can afford making inferior, time-wasting moves like 4. Nxd5 and 5. Qf3, and still get "only" slightly worse position. Still, if I want to play for a draw against a superior opponent (World Champion

*Vishy Anand or perhaps Rybka)
I'd prefer to do it from a position
of strength (3. d4, 3. Bb5+ Bd7 4.
Be2 +/=) rather than from a position of weakness (5. Qf3=/+).*

5. ... c6
I can initiate a queen trade
without developing an opponent's piece? Hmmm, let me see
...

*I'd prefer 5. ... Be6, prepar-
ing to castle long. Still, after 5. ...
c6 (or 5. ... e6) Black is better,
too.*

**6. Qxd5 cxd5 7. d4 Nc6 8.
Bb5 Bf5**

9. Bxc6+ bxc6
*Yet another concession.
Black's advantage grows.*
**10. c3 e6 11. Nf3 Bd6 12.
0-0**

12. ... 0-0
OK, both sides have castled.
I'm one move behind on development. The b-file is open, but I
can play b3 if necessary. Opponent has the bishop pair, which
can be a strong weapon. Erasing
one of his bishops would be nice.
*When in the endgame, do not
rush to castle! Your king might be
both safe (often) and more effi-
cient (always) staying closer to
the center. Black should play here
12. ... f6, followed by ... Kf7 and
perhaps ... g5, later preparing either ... c5 or even ... e5.*
**13. Re1 c5 14. dxc5 Bxc5 15.
Ne5**

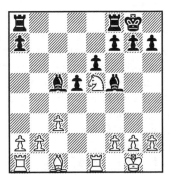

Looking to a fork on d7.

15. ... Rfd8

So much for that idea.

16. Be3 Bxe3 17. Rxe3

That was a good bishop exchange on general principles because it breaks up the bishop pair. Because of the rook, I did not have to isolate the f-pawn by fxe3.

17. ... d4 18. cxd4 Rxd4 19. Nc6

Threatening his rook and looking to a fork on e7.

Excellent!

19. ... Rd7

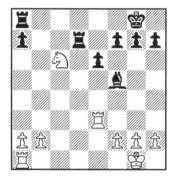

Again my 1750+ rated opponent sees it and foils it.

Black's uninspired play (12. ... 0-0) resulted in a practically equal position — after, say, the solid 20. h3 or the sharper 20. b4. Moving the knight back is less logical, but not too bad either.

20. Ne5 Rd2

21. b3

Relieving the threat and creating an outpost at c4.

21. ... Rad8 22. Ree1 f6 23. Nc4 R2d7 24. Ne3

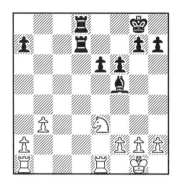

Attacking the bishop and defending d1 so I can run rooks over to that square.

24. ... Bd3 25. Red1

OK, I'm set. Locked on to the rooks on d-file.

25. ... Kf7

Supporting his rooks and looking ahead to the endgame.

26. f3

Also looking ahead to an endgame.

26. ... Ke7

Supporting his rooks.

An attractive alternative was 26. ... e5 followed by 27. ... Ke6 — CENTRALIZATION!

27. Kf2 Bc2

I have to be really careful about move order here.

28. Rxd7+ Rxd7 29. Nxc2

Yes, I did this with the advance knowledge that Rd2+ was coming.

29. ... Rd2+ 30. Kg3 Rxc2

31. h3

Stronger is the immediate 31. a4.

31. ... f5

After 31. ... Rb2! White's best would have been a pawn sac, 32. Rc1, with a likely — but not easy to achieve — draw.

32. a4 *(! — L.A.)*

Permitting my rook to leave a1.

32. ... Rb2

This may be the error that allows me to advance toward a draw. Opponent's objective may have been to force me to trap my own rook on a3 to defend b3, but I play ...

33. Rc1

(! — L.A.)

If 33. ... Rxb3, I can play 34. Rc7+ and erase the a-pawn, thereby creating a passer for me on the a-file.

33. ... Kd7

Black continues to play timidly. Why not 33. ... Kd6, for instance?

34. Rc3 e5

Pushing to an endgame.

Rather, to a bad endgame. Black is still better after 34. ... g5.

35. Rc5

Offering up an exchange.

An excellent move. White is already better.

35. ... Rxb3 36. Rxe5

This exchange nullifies the pawn majorities on both sides and makes this a more drawish game.

Not at all drawish.

36. ... g6 37. Ra5

This is the beginning of my drawn-endgame strategy. My opponent will be forced to trap his rook on the seventh rank, while my command of space on the fifth rank will prevent any advance by Black's king.

All good, but why should it be a drawn endgame strategy? White is clearly better; let's make Black show that he knows how to draw.

37. Rb7 38. Kh4

Or 38. Ra6!?, cutting off the Black king.

38. ... Ke6

My opponent could've pushed h7-h6 here to keep me from penetrating his pawn structure. Then ... Ke6 could've come later.

38. ... h6 is met by 39. Ra6.

39. Kg5 Kd6 40. g4 fxg4

Decision time? Not really, since I'm already playing for a draw. The move hxg4 would leave both sides open to an exchange leading to passed pawns. fxg4 tends to lock up all the kingside pawns.

41. fxg4

I play the drawish fxg4.

Wrong attitude. Why not raise

your goals in changed circum-stances? Both 41. fxg4 and 41. hxg4 are drawish in a sense that White can't lose — but Black can, and should.

41. ... Re7 42. Kh6 Ke6 43. h4

43. ... Kf6

Another decision. Pushing g5 is a check that gives me another move, but it boxes in my king. Pushing h4-h5 leads to an exchange and furthers my drawish agenda.

44. h5 gxh5 45. Kxh5 Rg7

Despite White's peaceful in-tentions, he is still winning, and the road to victory is both simple and without any risk of losing. After 46. g5+ Ke6 47. Kh6 White wins by playing Rb5, (a4)-a5-a6 and then Rb7, a line also pre-ferred by Rybka. Another plan, bringing the White rook to h8, is also always very promising, and risk-free.

46. Kh4 Re7, draw.

I offer a draw at this point and my opponent accepts. He did not have a winning solution and he was under two minutes on the clock. *(! — L.A.)* Drawing a 1750+ player is terrific, and it il-lustrates perhaps the one disad-vantage for the higher player in these early-round Swiss mis-matches. The lower-rated player has a strong motive to play for a draw, so he can play drawish moves that frustrate the higher-rated opponent.

Of course, it wasn't too late to repeat the position, and win (see my previous comment). I hope many readers will find helpful the various rook endings discussed above. I also like to thank my friend NM Jon Crumiller for his help with this game. Jon loves rook endings and understands them as a true grandmaster.

Part IX
Time Management and Other Useful Thinking Techniques

Game 37: Managing Time

Analyzing a chess game not knowing the time spent on each move is like making a medical diagnosis via telephone! In both cases, the information is probably incomplete.

Why is a Master so much stronger than a C-player? Because: (a) he knows more; (b) he knows things which are truly important; (c) his knowledge is active — i.e., ready to be used in a game; (d) he thinks more effectively, and (e) last but not least, he allocates his time better. This last element is often ignored by club players. In submissions to my column, time is mentioned very rarely, and then only as in "he was short of time" or "my time was running out, so I accepted a draw offer."

Kevin Funderburk played an interesting, instructive game, and accompanied it with thoughtful annotations. But I'll try to show that information about the time spent on certain moves is badly needed — and missing.

Writes Kevin:

My name is Kevin Funderburk and I am an unrated player. My first experience with chess was about six years ago as a teen. Getting severely thrashed, repeatedly, quickly lost its appeal. I have only recently taken to chess with more enthusiasm; a year and a half ago, to be exact. *Pandolfini's Endgame Course*

(an excellent choice! — LA) and a few issues of *Chess Life* have been my only tutors in the last eighteen months. Needless to say, I can't wait to add to that repertoire.

Queen's Gambit Declined
[D35]
White: Kevin Funderburk
(Unrated)
Black: Big Forty (Unrated)

1. d4 d5 2. c4

2. ... Nf6
This Marshall Defense surrenders the center — and favors White after 3. cxd5!

After
3. cxd5

3. ... Nxd5 (or 3. ... Qxd5 4. Nc3 Qa5 5. Bd2. If 5. ... Qb6, then 6. Nf3, and the b2-pawn is pure poison; 6. ... Qxb2?? 7. Rb1 Qa3 8. Nb5, winning) 4. e4 (Also good is 4. Nf3 Bf5 5. Nbd2, with a clear edge) 4. ... Nf6 5. f3, maintaining the central duo (After the natural 5. Nc3 e5! 6. Nf3! exd4 7. Qxd4 White's advantage is smaller).

Finally — and importantly — if Black wanted to get the position after his third move (as in the game), he had to play 2. ... e6 (first) and only then, on Move 3, ... Nf6. Kevin, however, didn't exploit Black's inferior second move (I suspect he played his 3. Nc3 very quickly).

3. Nc3 e6

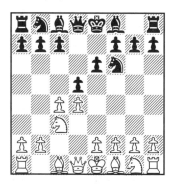

I've played this opening several times, both as White and as Black, with favorable results.

4. e3 Be7

Black usually plays 4... Bb4.

White's 4. e3 is a relatively rare move — not bad, but not as ambitious as the more common 4. Bg5, 4. Nf3 or 4. cxd5. By blocking his dark-square bishop, White practically gives up his opening edge. Black can equalize with either 4. ... c5 or 4. ... Be7 (as in the game), while 4. ... Bb4 transfers into a main line Nimzo-Indian. A question I would have asked a student: how long did you think before playing 4. e3, and what were you thinking about?

5. Nf3 0-0 6. Bd3

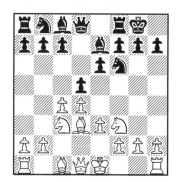

6... Nc6

In double queen-pawn openings (1. d4 d5) it's usually not good to block the neighboring c-pawn with a knight — unless that knight enables (soon!) the central thrust e4 (for White) or ... e5 (for Black). Black should have played here 6. ... b6 or 6. ... c5, with approximate equality.

7. a3

The move 7. 0-0 might have been better but I did not want Black's knight to threaten my bishop,. I had early plans of attack on Black's kingside with the light-color bishop taking a key role.

I like 7. a3. Among other things, it keeps Black's c6-knight in its current — pawn-blocking — position.

7. ... Ng4??

Big blunder! Not only is this move useless but it wastes a tempo once I push my h-pawn.

8. h3 Nh6

This appears to be another blunder by Black. The knight seems to be misplaced here. When I saw this move, I immediately saw a potential target for my dark bishop which would seriously cripple Black's kingside, should it remain.

9. 0-0

*After several bad and dubious moves by Black, Kevin should expect to be (much) better, but how to take advantage of the situa-*tion? *It's not that obvious, and it requires, in a tournament game, 15-20 minutes of deliberation. The move Kevin made, 9. 0-0, guarantees White an advantage after, say, 9. ... dxc4 10. Bxc4 Nf5.*

Can we try for more? Can we bury the knight on h6? Not that easy, as 9. g4 is met by 9. ... dxc4 10. Bxc4 f5, with a counterplay — or if 9. cxd5 exd5 10. g4, than also 10. ... f5. Perhaps White should simply win a pawn: 9. cxd5 exd5 10. Qb3 Be6 11. Qxb7, and because of Black's "exiled" h6-knight, Black gets no full compensation for a lost pawn.

9. ... b6?

Better was 9. ... Nf5. The game move allows me to exploit the misplaced knight and weaken his kingside.

Not so. If 9. ... Nf5, 10. Bxf5, winning a pawn. Relatively better is 9. ... dxc4 10. Bxc4 Nf5.

10. e4 dxe4 11. Bxe4 Bb7

12. Bxh6 gxh6 13. d5 exd5 14. cxd5 Na5

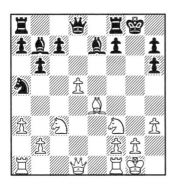

15. Ne5
*Or 15. Nd4!?, preventing ...
f5. Note how vulnerable is the
black king — and Black's a5-
knight.*
15. ... Bf6??

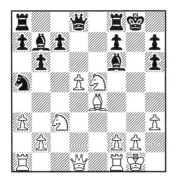

This was the final mistake.
Black needed the ugly 15. ... f5 to
stop the immediate mate. 15. ...
f5 16. Bc2 *(or 16. Bxf5 Rxf5 17.
Qg4+ Rg5 18. Qe6+ Kg7 19. f4
Rxe5 20. fxe5, with a strong attack — L.A.)*
16. ... Ba6 17. Re1. Things are
still not going good for Black.
White clearly has the better position. Now neither 17. ... Nc4 nor

17. ... Nb7 are good, both met by
18. Nc6.
16. Qh5
After I made this move, I realized I just prolonged the mate
unnecessarily: 16. Qg4+ Bg5 17.
Qf5 followed by mate. By going
16. Qh5 I just delayed the inevitable — 16. ... Kg7 17. Qg4+
Bg5 18. Qf5 and Black cannot
stop it. But Black decided to
speed things up in order to attempt retribution all the more
quickly in the next game.
*After 16. Qh5? Bxe5! White is
much better, but the game is far
from over (time spent on 16. Qh5
— alas, unknown).*
16. ... Qe7 17. Qxh6 Rfe8

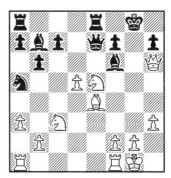

**18. Bxh7+, and Black re-
signed.**
*If 18. ... Kh8, then 19. Bg6+
Kg8 20. Bxf7+.*
My opponent made too many
errors and it cost him. Please for-
give my Novice notes. I am an
amateur player and still quite
new to chess, though I hope to
improve. I always try to learn

from others' games so perhaps with this example, another may as well.

I definitely think so.

One of the key elements of chess mastery is the ability to use your chess time efficiently. By "chess time" I don't mean "chessic time," a.k.a. development/ tempi, but time on your chess clock and time spent on each move. I strongly suggest to those who want to improve their play — quickly — to start paying attention to this critical component of the chess game.

Whenever you play a "normal time control" game (30/90+SD/1, or 40/120+SD/1) — write down the time left on both clocks after every move made any time there is more than one minute thinking time (stop writing when you get in time pressure, of course).

Later, analyze the game paying attention to the time spent on each move. You'll undoubtedly discover that many mistakes were caused by playing too quickly in situations where long thought was called for. Soon you'll learn to recognize such situations.

Quick summary of the game, highlighting critical moments:

Black's inaccuracy on Move 2 / White allows it to go unpunished.

On Move 4, White chooses an unambitious 4. e3.

Black blocks the c-pawn on Move 6; White stands better as a result

White's 7. a3 — a praiseworthy prophylaxis.

Black, on Move 7, starts time-wasting maneuvers which lands his knight on the (bad) h6 square.

White misses a chance to win a pawn on Move 9; still, he's clearly better.

White takes on h6 (on Move 12, after starting it all with 10. e4), damaging Black's king's pawn cover.

On the 15th move, in a clearly worse position, Black blunders — but then White misses a forced win (discovered by Kevin in post-mortem analysis — good for him!).

On the 16th move, Black missed his last (just given) chance to prolong the play with 16. ... Bxe5 (not in Kevin's notes — still room for improvement!), and resigns on the next move, as his position is lost by now.

Game 38: Blitz!

Everybody loves blitz. Millions of blitz games are played daily — in clubs, parks, and on the Net — by players ranging from beginners to world champions. Clearly, blitz is, for most of us, enjoyable. But is it helpful?

Michael Botvinnik thought blitz contributes to our natural tendency to make "natural" (and sometimes superficial) moves. Thus, he never played blitz, and advised others against it.

Most GMs, however, have a more nuanced, indeed a more favorable, view of blitzing. Botvinnik's own students, world champions Karpov, Kasparov, and Kramnik, are among the best in five-minute chess.

Yes, blitz alone can be detrimental to your chess growth, but combined with some serious play, blitz is OK. After all, blitz exposes you to thousands of new positions in just a few hours; trains your intuition, decisiveness, mastery of time, and short-term combination skills. To train other important qualities, such as in-depth calculation, deep strategic thinking, and planning — look for longer time controls.

Our contributor Dr. Gary Axelson raises some interesting, practical questions about blitz in his letter.

First a brief note of appreciation for **Chess Openings for Black**, which I received as a gift over the holidays. The format is wonderful and the content very useful. I haven't given up my love of the derelict Scandinavian Defense (which I was glad to see received good press from you and your co-authors), but I have taken on the Accelerated Dragon as a second Black line. I had tried it once upon a time, but got wary about dealing with the Maroczy Bind. Your treatment of the rich opening cured me.

Now then, down to Basics. I've enclosed a game both as an example of and as a springboard for some questions about the basics of Blitz. The game was played this past fall on the ChessBase server, Playchess. com.

The five minute clock changes play dramatically and seems guaranteed to promote time pressure errors which are nightmares if you're the blunderer. And then, even when behind, there is always the chance that your opponent will return the favor, make his or her own gaffe, and let you right back in. In any case, I am hoping that you might devote a column to the do's and don'ts on playing blitz. How do you manage your clock when you play it, do you pick offbeat openings to make your opponents spend clock time figuring out where the landmines are, what other things do you do or avoid in a way that is different from your play in a standard time control game? And should you limit the amount of Blitz you play — that is, does too much of it ruin you for tournament chess?

Anyhow, whether you choose my game or not, I hope you will consider the topic.

My replies/comments:

a) the best way to excel in blitz is to excel in chess. With very few exceptions, world-class players are also world-class in blitz (Capablanca, Tal, Petrosian, Fischer, Nakamura, to name just a few). Only a few masters can compete with strong GMs in blitz. One of them was Henrich Chepukaitis from Petersburg (Russia) who also wrote an excellent book on how to excel in blitz.

b) Manage the clock the same way you would do in any Sudden Death time control (another way that blitz benefits "real" chess). Try not to fall too far behind your opponent in time — unless you're searching for a mate, a perpetual check or a dead-draw ending.

c) Playing offbeat openings does make sense — but so does

playing your "normal" openings, achieving positions which you know and which you, equally importantly, understand well.

d) At last one difference to note: in blitz, the value of the initiative (vs. the material) grows. Be ready to sac a pawn even if it is bringing you only half a pawn worth of initiative!

Danish Gambit [C44]
White: Gary Axelson
Black: Guest

1. e4 e5 2. Nf3 Nc6 3. d4 exd4 4. c3 dxc3 5. Bc4 cxb2 6. Bxb2

6. ... Nh6

"Guest" must have been reading *My System*, but this wasn't what Nimzovich had in mind. Black overprotects his f7 pawn, expecting a bishop sac. But f7 wasn't in jeopardy yet — and the knight is now sitting out in the parking lot.

ECO *here recommends 6. ... d6, with an unclear position, quoting Ljubojevic-Smeikal, 1972.*

7. 0-0 f6

The move 7. … d6 was better here, but Guest intends to protect his f7 square at all costs. Let's review the bidding. Black is up two whole pawns. But deals that look to good to be true, usually are. Black's king is stuck in the center. He is cramped and underdeveloped. White has space and development and good prospects to bring some unwanted company into Black's home. And all the relatives.

8. e5

Ringing the doorbell.

8. … Be7 9. exf6 Bxf6 10. Re1+ Ne7

10. … Kf8 was Black's best try.

11. Ne5

Rude intentions, but with the blitz clock ticking totally missing the ruder, in fact totally impolite 11. Bxf6 gxf6 12. Ng5

After 12. Ng5

12. … fxg5 13. Qh5+ Kf8 14. Qxh6+ Ke8 15. Qh5+ Kf8 16. Qf7, mate.

11. … d6?

What was needed here was 11. … d5, to slam the door in my face.

12. Qh5+

12. … Ng6??

A second mistake while the clock relentlessly counts down. Fortunately the time pressure mutes Black's judgment too!

13. Nxg6+ Kd7

14. Nxh8

Now Fritz shows a very pretty mate in ten, starting with 14. Be6+, but this is blitz and I'm not a Master (maybe some day if I keep reading books!)

14. Be6+ Ke8 15. Bxc8+ Kf7 16. Be6+ Ke8 17. Bd5+ Qe7 18. Nxe7+ Kd7 19. Qh3+ Ke8 20. Ng8+ Kf8 21. Nxf6 Nf7 22. Qd7 Ne5 23. Bxe5 gxf6 24. Qf7, mate.

You don't need to calculate many moves ahead to play 14. Be6+. Already the first reply — 14. ... Ke8 (if 14. ... Kc6, then 15. Qd5+, as in the game) allows White to capture, with check, the c8-bishop, and then the queen (all moves, importantly, being checks.) Simply play 14. Be6+ and then think on the opponent's time.

14. ... Bxb2

He thought he had me here, but no worries. White has the firepower and the space to make things work out.

15. Be6+ Kc6 16. Qf3+

Yes, Qd5+ would have been better.

16. ... Kb6

Tick tock tick tock. The clock bails me out from an imprecision once again.

Even the stronger 16. ... d5 wasn't sufficient: 17. Nc3!, and White's attack against the wandering king is decisive.

17. Qb3+ Ka6 18. Bc4+

And with mate coming in one more move, **Black resigns.**

Sloppy play by me here and there which would have been punished by a stronger opponent or a slower time control. On the other hand, I would have never played a Goring Gambit at a standard time control. I'd be back in my grey flannel, button-down London system, with lots of safety. But I probably would have had a whole lot less fun, too. This was like a great roller coaster ride!

Game 39:
The Psychic Powers of the Queen

Many chessplayers subconsciously treat a queen as if her value is almost unlimited — and act accordingly.
This often leads to mistakes and to missed opportunities.

Our contributor, Edward Guzman, like many other players I know, returned to serious chess after a long, long hiatus. Writes Edward:

When I started playing chess in 1986, I learned the moves and played occasionally with friends. Twenty years passed by before I resumed playing with intent to master it. It has been a difficult road, for time is very limited and you have to make ends meet. I have become very serious about learning this game well enough to play in tournaments. I have bought several books on openings, middlegames, and endings, but books without practice are futile. I participated in my first real tournament this year, the World Open 2007 in the Under-1400 class. I didn't do that well. Participated in a couple of local tournaments at the Marshall Club. I did okay. Now I have joined the Commercial Chess League of New York (CCLNY) with some friends for the practice and to have some fun.

After losing round one our Bryant Park team has managed to win three straight matches with some excellent play from our players. So we are back in contention. This time I was paired against a stronger player rated 300+ points higher. My opponent played some kind of queen's pawn opening, perhaps to throw me off mentally. As I mentioned previously, this is not uncommon in many of the games I have witnessed lately. But occasionally this strategy has backfired.

Queen's Pawn Opening [D03]
White: Bob Leonards (1767)
Black: Edward Guzman (1442)
2007

1. d4 d5 2. Nf3 Nf6 3. Bg5 e6 4. e3 Nbd7 5. Bd3

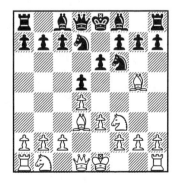

5. ... c6
I was expecting 6. c4 on the

next move, going into the Queen's Gambit, with which I'm very familiar. But no!

I'd prefer here 5. ... Be7, preserving an option to play ... c7-c5 in one move.

6. c3 Qb6 7. Qc2 Bd6

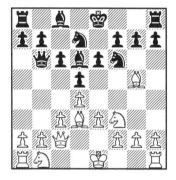

Developing the bishop this way is best.

8. Nd2 h6

See what he intends to do. I don't think he likes my bishop controlling the h2-b8 diagonal.

9. Bh4 0-0

My development is almost complete. I need to develop my queen bishop quickly.

10. Bg3 c5!

The best move. It protects the bishop, and, if White takes on c5, re-taking with the knight allows me to develop the bishop to d7; and then my rooks take control of the c-line.

Correct. Thus, White should not take on c5 now. Better is 11. 0-0, later preparing e4.

11. dxc5 Nxc5 12. Be2 Bd7

My development is complete. No doubt, Black is better.

13. Bxd6 Qxd6

So far it's all Black.

14. 0-0

14. ... Rac8

As prescribed, rooks belong on open and/or semi-open lines. *(Usually referred to as "files" — LA)*

15. Rad1

Better was 15. Rac1, preparing either c4 or (after Qb1) Nb3.

15. ... Qc7

No need to rush the queen out, but sooner or later it has to move. Safety first!

16. Nb3? Ba4!

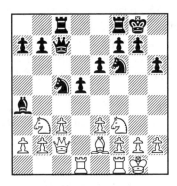

This pin should not have been allowed. But White hasn't many good moves anyway!

17. Nfd2 Rfd8

Notice the cramping of White's position, while Black continues developing.

Better 17. ... Qb6, piling on a pinned knight.

18. f3 Qe5

This wins a pawn at h2 but I decided against it. Taking the pawn would allow White to gain uncontested access to the h-line.

19. Kf2

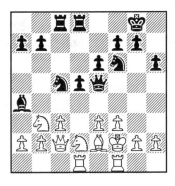

19. ... Qg5

It took me about 10 minutes

to decide on this move. I wanted to take advantage of the rook x-ray on the queen on the c-line and have been considering the d4 pawn push for several moves. The e5 and d4 pawn moves while the White king is in the middle of the board looks very attractive at the moment.

Edward's thoughtful (10 minutes! — very good) decision was, alas, wrong. Black should grab the h-pawn, as White can't use the h-file in any meaningful way. Thus, Black enjoys all his other advantages — plus an extra pawn.

20. Rfe1 d4!

Black overestimates his position, and his plan. The root cause of his problems is, as we'll see, the over-valuing of the queen.

21. exd4 Rxd4!

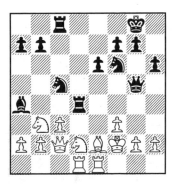

22. Nf1

White spent about 15 or so minutes on this move. I am ahead now on time by 30+ minutes.

Of course, White cannot take or else he will lose material.

Main variation: 22. cxd4 Nce4+

After
22. ...
Nce4+

23. Nxe4 Qh4+ 24. Ng3 Rxc2
and wins.

*Look at the analysis diagram.
There 23. Qxe4! leaves White
with extra material after 23. ...
Nxe4 24. Nxe4.*

After
24. Nxe4

*White has a rook and two
minor pieces for a queen; even
after Black wins a pawn, perhaps
even two (which he should), material and the position would be
approximately equal.*

*Don't, however, limit yourself
to simply counting material, and
don't underestimate the queen either especially if she acts to-
gether with several other
remaining pieces and if the opponent's king is vulnerable, or
open to checks, and some of the
opponent's men are loose.*

22. ... Rf4

23. Kg1

After having spent a lot of
time in the previous move, White
made this move quickly, 23. g3
might have offered better
chances to hold the position.

Correct.

23. ... Nd5

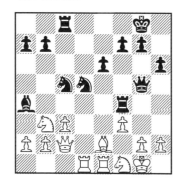

24. Bd3?

The move 24. g3 which weakens the kingside, or 24. Qd2
which loses at least a pawn, are
probably better choices.

*I like the aggressive g3 now
and on a previous move. 24. Bd3
(the game) is a losing blunder. In
fact, White was doing fine — an-*

other proof why both 19. ... Qg5 and 20. ... d4 were too optimistic/unrealistic.

24. ... Rxf3! 25. Be4 Rxf1!+

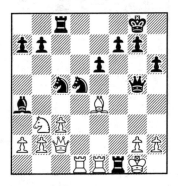

26. Rxf1 Ne3

This is decisive.

27. Qf2 Nxe4

There is no rush in taking either rook – they are going nowhere. Now I am a piece ahead.

28. Qxf7+ Kh8 29. Qxb7 Qxg2, mate

Game 40:
How to Beat a Grandmaster

Playing in time pressure, even the strongest players have to make superficial moves — and often can't afford to check, far less double-check, their first choices. Still, it requires good play to take advantage of an opponent's inaccuracies, good play which was demonstrated by my opponent, Jim Joline.

We spoke recently at the U.S. Amateur Team East in New Jersey. You autographed my book, and I mentioned that I had played in your simultaneous exhibition at Hazelton, Pennsylvania, some years ago. (To my surprise, the year we played was 1990!) Here I submit that game for your enjoyment.

It remains the high point of my chess life. Because you're a grandmaster, I kept expecting lightning to strike from high above the board, at some point during the game, and sweep my position onto the floor. I've taken the liberty of interjecting a few recollections, which I had written down after reviewing the game at home.

The local newspaper covered the event, and finding that I'd won my game, interviewed me on the assumption that I must be some sort of genius. In simuls, the time disparity itself is enough, but you also had some 30 other contenders pitted against you.

I realize I could not have done what I did against you one-on-one. *(A B-player's chances of drawing, not to say beating, a grandmaster are small, but not infinitesmal. In the U.S. Open 1985, I lost a first-round game to an 1860 player [and still tied for 2nd-3rd] — L.A.).* Please accept this game, knowing that it remains one of my most treasured memories.

Two Knights' Defense [C57]
White: GM Lev Alburt
Black: Jim Joline (1667)
Hazelton simul, 1990

1. e4 e5 2. Nf3 Nc6 3. Bc4 Nf6 4. Ng5 d5 5. exd5

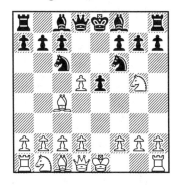

5. ... Nxd5

Black's last move is the most natural and the oldest, but not the strongest, response. Best is 5. ... Na5 (also more than a century old), while the more modern 5. ... Nd4 or even 5. ... b5 are also playable.

6. d4 exd4

7. Nxf7?!

An erroneous mixing of the two different lines; a move earlier, 6. Nxf7 led to a complicated, unclear game; the point of 6. d4 is to follow with 7. 0-0, and White stands better. I overlooked Black's strong reply.

7. ... Qe7+ 8. Qe2 Qxe2+

Getting the queens off early is good for Black.

9. Kxe2

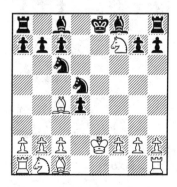

9. ... d3+

If Black takes the knight now with Kxf7, then 10. Bxd5+ Be6 11. Bxc6 breaks Black's pawns.

I planned, after 9. ... Kxf7 10. Bxd5+ Bxe6+, to take on e6 and fight for equality. After 11. Bxc6 bxc6 Black is better, thanks to his unopposed strong light-squared bishop and his advantage in the center.

10. Kxd3

A serious error. After 10. cxd3 Nd4+ 11. Kd2 (or 11. Kd1) 11. ... Kxf7 12. Bxd5+ Black is okay, perhaps even somewhat better, but White at least has a pawn to suffer for. After 10. Kxd3 there is no extra pawn, only suffering.

10. ... Ncb4+ 11. Kd2 Kxf7 12. a3 Be6 13. axb4 Bxb4+ 14. c3 Bc5

15. b4?

Another tempting superficial move — in a position where White hangs by a thread and must play very accurately , and creatively, to survive. Perhaps 15. Re1 offered the best chances to hold on.

15. ... Bb6

The move ... Bxf2 loses the bishop to Rf1.

16. f3

Not a must (the pawn isn't hanging yet) but what else is there to do? After 16. Kc2 Nxb4+ the negative consequences of the "natural" 15. b4 become apparent. Perhaps 16. Na3 was the best defense.

16. ... Rad8 17. Bxd5 Bxd5 18. Kc2 Rhe8 19. Nd2 Re2

Black's simple and powerful moves 16 through 19 clinch a win.

20. g3 Be3

Preparing to win the knight on d2, after 20. ... Bc4.

21. Kd1 Bxf3

22. Kc2

If now 22. Rf1 then 22. ... Rexd2++ 23. Ke1 Rd1 mate.

22. ... Bxh1, White resigns.

In June of 1990, my USCF rating was 1667. I have never been able to maintain a stable rating — it has always been subject to great fluctuation because I don't concentrate well under pressure. So you can understand why I treasure this game as I do.

I think the only real instructional value in it is the idea of development with tempo to control the center. And I know you would not have played as you did in a serious game. Thanks for the gift.

This wasn't exactly a gift — Black earned his win. Still, I am glad this game provides an inspiration for Jim, as it will, I hope, for many other readers of this book. May you all win many games to treasure!

How to Beat a Grandmaster

1. Play your "normal" chess game.
2. In particular, play your usual opening lines.
3. Be inspired, not intimidated.
4. Try to recall your best performances and live up to them.
5. Avoid unnecessary complications and uncertainties, but ...
6. Go for complications when the position requires. In this case ...
7. Don't be lazy; think for a long time before making an important decision and calculate as many variations as you need (or can).
8. Remember, Grandmasters make mistakes (albeit rarely), especially when they are short of time — for instance, when giving a simul. Therefore, ...
9. Be alert. Watch for an opportunity and be ready to grab it (you may not get a second chance.)

Index of Games

It's Easy to Order Books
from Lev Alburt!

Vol. 1

Learn Chess in 12 Lessons
126 pp.
$16 ⁹⁵

A Fresh Look at Chess

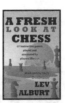

40 instructive games, played and annotated by players like you.
224 pp.
$17⁹⁵

Chess for the Gifted and Busy
304 pp.
$19⁹⁵

Vol. 2

From Beginner to Tournament Player
304 pp.
$28⁹⁵

Pirc Alert!

A Complete Defense Against 1. e4
448 pp.
$34⁹⁵

Chess Openings for Black, Explained
552 pp.
$29.95

Vol. 3

Chess Tactics for the Tournament Player
246 pp.
$19⁹⁵

Building Up Your Chess
352 pp.
$29⁹⁵

Vol. 4

The King in Jeopardy: Attack and Defense
256 pp.
$19⁹⁵

Chess Rules of Thumb
192 pp.
$19⁹⁵

Chess Openings for White, Explained
548 pp.
$29.95

Vol. 5

Chess Strategy for the Tournament Player
356 pp.
$24⁹⁵

Please see order forms on pages 223 & 224 or go to www.chesswithlev.com

Vol. 6

Chess Training Pocketbook: 300 Most Important Positions and Ideas
188 pp.
17⁹⁵

Three Days with Bobby Fischer
288 pp.
$29⁹⁵

Vol. 7

Just the Facts! Winning Endgame Knowledge in One Volume
412 pp.
$26⁹⁵

Vol. 8

Chess Training Pocket Book II
320 Key Positions
208 pp.
18⁹⁵

Three Days with Bobby Fischer
288 pp.
$29⁹⁵

It's Easy to Order Books from Lev Alburt!

New! Order Online Using Credit Cards or PayPal!
Get complete information on all books, find out how to get personal lessons, and watch free instructional videos!

www.chesswithlev.com
or call Lev directly at 212.794.8706

It's Easy to Order Books from Lev Alburt!

New! Order Online Using Credit Cards or PayPal!

Get complete information on all books, find out how to get
personal lessons, and watch free instructional videos!

www.chesswithlev.com

or call Lev directly at 212.794.8706